Her Thorns

*When Pain Paves the Way
for Healing*

JORDYN IMARI

For the people who are hurting.
May your wounds heal fully from the touch of Holy hands.
May your heart feel whole again.
May you find joy again.
May you find peace again.
May you rest in the assurance that Jesus hears you, sees you,
and loves you.

Contents

Introduction

"...So to keep me from becoming proud, I was given a thorn in my flesh, a messenger from Satan to torment me and keep me from becoming proud. Three different times I begged the Lord to take it away. Each time he said, 'My grace is all you need. My power works best in weakness.' So now I am glad to boast about my weaknesses, so that the power of Christ can work through me" (2 Corinthians 12:7-9, New Living Translation).

Her Thorns started as the pages of my journals. My journals have seen some of my darkest moments, and God instructed me to put them all together as a book. Ever since I was a little girl, I have wanted to be a writer, but my life didn't look like it was headed that way; I got a degree in Speech Pathology instead. Even though I hated what I was studying, I kept going because I thought "my plan" was the safest route.

However, God wrecked all my plans during my senior year of college. He told me that He never wanted me to pursue speech therapy but to pursue writing. He needed me to get back in His will for my life, and writing for His glory was my path. I earned a bachelor's degree that I never used and incurred a lot of debt. However, I knew what God was calling me to do. So, I took a leap of faith, completely afraid yet trusting God. He opened the door for me to go to graduate school for free and pursue writing. Even though I still don't know all God wants me to do, I know He's in control, and obedience is always the right response to God.

I often tried not to write this book because it was too hard. I gave up on it for four years and started another book project that was easier and more comfortable to write. Then an opportunity came for me to publish this book, not the one I was working on. God gently said, "Finish the book." I knew exactly what book He was talking about.

As a reader, I hope to give you something to identify with. Too often, we feel like we are alone, and I want to offer encouragement. You are not alone. I have been in darkness, felt alone, wanted my life to end, and I have seen countless others deal with the same issues. I hope the words on these pages say everything you've been afraid to let out.

Through compassion, transparency, and love, I want to show you the One who has never failed me. I hope to show you His love and grace. I don't know who this book is intended for, and I certainly don't know who it'll reach, but I pray the outpouring of my heart can ease the aching of the thorns in your side.

Important note: This serves as a trigger warning. This book contains vivid accounts of emotional, physical, and sexual abuse, as well as suicide attempts. All character names have been changed, and written permission has been obtained to preserve the confidentiality of the victims.

Chapter 1

The Couch

Have you ever been so scared that you felt your heart drop into your stomach? Imagine that feeling right now. It was an ordinary Sunday morning, and I was upstairs getting dressed for church. While listening to gospel music, I thought I heard a painful moan. I paused to listen but thought maybe my ears were hearing things. I resumed getting dressed, and then I heard it again. I knew someone was groaning, and it sounded much like my name. I nervously walked downstairs to investigate the sound. Every horror movie I have ever seen popped into my mind as I slowly descended the stairs. When I rounded the corner in the kitchen, I saw my sister, Zoie, lying in a puddle of vomit.

"I think I need to go to the hospital," Zoie said painfully. Her eyes glossed over as she cried, clenching her stomach.

"What's wrong?" I asked in a worried tone. "Are you sick?"

"I took 13 of Mom's pills," she said as she looked at me with sorrow in her eyes.

I stared at her for a moment in utter disbelief. Did I hear that correctly? One million questions ran through my head as I scrambled to rush her to the hospital. One of the first things I felt was anger. I was angry that she would try to take her own life. What if I had found her dead? How would that have affected me? In retrospect, I realize these were selfish questions, but at the time, they were all I had. I also had an overwhelming feeling of sadness. I wondered why my sister hadn't come to me if she was struggling this badly. As her big sister, I felt like a colossal failure, but there was no time to think about that. I helped her into the car and drove to the hospital like Zoie's life depended on it — because it did.

When I arrived at the emergency room with Zoie, the intake team would not let me check her in initially because I wasn't her parent. I looked at the medical assistant square in her eyes and said, "You need to admit her. I'm not going anywhere until you do." She could tell I wasn't kidding, and they took Zoie to the back. I sighed with relief because I'm not usually one to be stern with anyone. But this was different.

My family met me at the hospital, and we all gathered in the waiting room. Some family members speculated this was all for attention, which disgusted me. My heart completely shattered for Zoie. I desperately wanted her to know that I was here for her and that she wasn't alone. My family and I waited nervously for someone to tell us she would be okay.

The doctor finally came out to the waiting room and informed us that Zoie had taken antibiotics from my mom's medicine cabinet, so they just upset her stomach. She would've died if it had been anything else or if she had taken any more. Following this incident, Zoie went to therapy for a few weeks. She was diagnosed with clinical depression and anxiety.

About six months later, it was like a gut-wrenching déjà vu. I received a spine-chilling call about my other sister, Simone.

Simone also took pills, attempting to end her life. After she took the pills, she sent a cryptic message to her husband and then drove to an abandoned parking lot to die. When my mom and stepdad found her, she was still breathing but hallucinating.

Again, I asked more selfish questions. What is wrong with my sisters? Why would Simone do this? Didn't she see how badly it scared us when Zoie attempted suicide? She has a daughter that needs her. Doesn't that mean anything to her?

Simone had a two-week stay in the psychiatric wing of the hospital. When I visited her, it felt like I had entered a prison. The staff made me lock my belongings up, and I wasn't allowed to have anything on me. I heard screams echoing down the hall from a woman refusing sedation. People stared at me as if I had two sets of eyes. I heard people talking to themselves and saw them rocking back and forth. It felt like I had just stepped onto a movie set.

I immediately thought that Simone didn't belong there. She didn't seem to have severe mental health issues like the other patients. Simone wasn't hearing things or hallucinating anymore. She wasn't having rapid mood swings or threatening to harm herself again. She seemed to be okay. But that wasn't the case. Just like Zoie, Simone felt so much sorrow that she wanted to take her own life.

By this time, my immediate family was the topic of gossip within our extended family. Everyone commented negatively on my sisters' suicide attempts and my mother's parenting. My family never openly discussed mental health issues, so misunderstandings and rumors spread like wildfire. Even after these incidents, we never discussed it. We went on with life as usual.

I couldn't wrap my head around the trauma I experienced

with my sisters for a while. I didn't have answers to any of the questions that lingered in my head. As a big sister, I felt I could have done a better job at seeing the signs and getting them help before they attempted to take their own lives. I blamed myself, but I also didn't understand what would make a person feel like they didn't want to live anymore, especially when they had so much to live for — until it was *me* in their shoes.

As counterintuitive as it sounds, healing hurts. It hurts before it does anything else. This is equally true for emotional wounds as it is for physical ones. When you get a cut, the first thing you feel is pain. The cut is the first step of healing. Without the cut and the pain, there would be nothing to heal or restore. We can try to avoid or run away from pain, but it has a funny way of showing back up if you don't deal with it the first time. Furthermore, it has an ugly way of manifesting in even worse forms than before. I would know.

Healing forces you to look at what's broken, and it's confusing. Some days it seems like rainbows and puppies; other days, it looks like a snotty nose and a tear-soaked pillow from crying so much your head hurts. One more thing about healing? If you actively seek it, you'll find it.

When my therapist, Ava, diagnosed me with clinical depression, anxiety, and Post Traumatic Stress Disorder (PTSD), I felt numb. Though the diagnosis finally put language to what I had been feeling for years, something about it felt uncomfortable. I thought only veterans struggled with PTSD, but I was wrong. People with PTSD look just like me.

I also thought depression was for ungrateful people. I used to be one of those "it could be worse" people. I thought about the children starving around the world or even families with food insecurity who lived up the street. I had all my necessities and then some. So how could I possibly be depressed? I've known for a while that I struggled with depression, but that didn't stop me from feeling guilty about the diagnosis. And clearly, it ran in my family.

My single mother raised two sisters and me in a Christian home. We followed the same weekly routine growing up: Church, school, repeat. We didn't talk about mental health, and we didn't have conversations about our emotions. My voice, opinions, and concerns weren't honored in my home, so this led to many pinned-up feelings and silent cries.

Growing up, struggling with mental illness meant you were dramatic and ungrateful. I would not have dared express that I was sad because what do kids have to be sad about? This was the thought process around mental illness in my home and community. This is especially true for black children, tragically following them into adulthood.

So, I sat there in therapy with utter confusion scribbled all over my face because I couldn't believe I was there, but I chose to seek healing despite my ignorance and reservations. To say I had a few bumps and bruises is an understatement. I think being run over by a car and then backed over four times more accurately describes how I felt. As I sat there on Ava's couch, I kept thinking about how I didn't want to be there. If I'm being completely honest, I went into therapy thinking, "Yay, healing," but then I quickly realized it wouldn't be easy or cheerful at all. It was going to be painful, challenging, and ugly. Most of us prefer to run in the opposite direction of pain. Therapy was forcing me to dive right in headfirst.

This was the first time I had ever experienced someone allowing me to talk about my pain. I never had professional help before. I never thought I *needed* professional help. After all, I was the child and sister who "had it all together."

I was the one people came to when they needed help. I was the one who usually always told everyone she was fine when the tears on her pillow told a much different story. I was broken, and a series of unfortunate events led me to where I was sitting that day — on my therapist's couch. Ava, my therapist, told me that my feelings were okay. As cliche as it sounds, hearing that my feelings were okay gave me hope I had never experienced before.

In our initial session, I held back a lot. I guess my facial expressions told the truth that my lips were too afraid to say. Being skilled at her job, Ava noticed that I wasn't expressing everything. I've never been good at controlling my facial expressions, so I'm not surprised they ratted me out. My eyes reflected the feelings I tried to suppress, and Ava called them out.

With that, she helped free me from the prison of other people's opinions. It was just Ava and me there, so I had nothing to fear. I didn't realize how much I made myself small to make others comfortable until I started therapy. I always stayed quiet about my hurt and let it eat me alive instead. Growing up, my mom labeled me the "overly sensitive child." So, I was taught very early on that I couldn't be honest about what hurt me. I feared being called dramatic.

"I'm afraid of being too much for people if I let everything out," I told Ava, trying to divert my eyes. I felt so embarrassed.

"And how has that been working for you? Keeping all your emotions in?" Ava asked me sincerely.

Her question pierced my heart and felt like a smack in the face, though I knew she didn't mean for it to hurt. It stung because we both knew the truth about why I was on her couch in the first place. I had tried to take my own life because "keeping everything in" became too much, and I didn't want to bear it anymore.

"Not good," I told her. "Not good at all."

I sat there feeling numb and disconnected. I felt embarrassed, ashamed, and worthless. I recalled the hurt in one of my friend's voices when she found out I didn't call for help before I attempted suicide. But, at that moment, my problem wasn't that I didn't *want* to call for help; I just felt like I *couldn't*. I felt no one would be there for me or understand my dark headspace. I felt like I'd be a bother to anyone who may have answered their phone—if they answered it at all. I felt like the girl who always had something wrong with her, and no one wanted to deal with me.

Every single negative thought that could have gone through my mind consumed me the first night I tried to take my own life. The lies in my head told me that maybe I got left out sometimes because I was the annoying friend. Or perhaps no one ever came to visit me because I wasn't a fun friend.

The devil fed me lies for breakfast, lunch, and dinner, and it worked. I believed every single one of those lies and wrapped a belt around my neck, draped it over the rod in my closet, and pulled it tighter and tighter, trying to escape the pain.

I thought this was it. I struggled to breathe and knew my body would soon be lifeless. I remember two things happening at that moment: A lightheaded feeling began to overtake me, but the other thing was a voice. As my eyes got heavy and began to shut, I heard a voice say, "One more day." Immediately, I loosened my grip on the belt around my neck. I was scared and hurting so badly, but I knew it was the Lord who spoke to me. He wanted one more day with me.

7

I wish I could say I felt better that night, but I didn't. My heart ached, and all I could do was cry myself to sleep. I lay on my pillow shaking and sobbing for hours. I felt so alone, but the Lord's words came again. "One more day" echoed in my head over and over. I honestly felt like I didn't have enough strength to give Him one more day, but clearly, He granted it to me; otherwise, you wouldn't be reading this book of healing.

"One more day" turned into many more days and another year. And with bumps and bruises all over me, here I am. I wish I could say the suicidal thoughts went away completely. I also wish I could say that was the last time I attempted to take my life, but that's not my story. I was frustrated with God because suicide seemed like the "thorn in my side." I told him I didn't understand why I felt so sad or why He wouldn't just take the pain away completely. Wasn't becoming a Christian supposed to end all this suffering? Or had I made the wrong choice in becoming a Christian? Maybe you've asked the same questions.

Mental illness has been a continuous struggle for me. However, I can confidently say that each time, God gently reminds me that I *can* handle another day because He's with me. He's in me. That's all I had to do — keep giving Him one more day.

If I've learned anything from my struggle with suicidal thoughts and attempts, it's that pain is real, and if it hurts you, it hurts you. No one gets to tell you something shouldn't hurt. I was allowed to be hurt. Rejection, abandonment, abuse, toxicity, depression, anxiety, inadequacy, and suicide all try to make themselves comfortable in my mind. Each time, I must call on the Lord for the strength to tell them that they aren't welcome. It has been difficult, but the Lord has proven Himself faithful, as He always does.

I had no idea when thoughts of ending my life became more

appealing than seeking God's purpose for it. I just know that one day, I thought about everything I had been through, and it resembled the valley of dry bones. I didn't like what I saw, and I didn't like who I was. My mental illness manifested in terrible ways. I hurt some important people, told some ugly lies, completely lost myself, and messed up in many ways. But for some reason, God loves me, and He loves you, too.

That was why I ended up in therapy — God asked me for another day. It wasn't much, but I had some fight left in me. I realized I didn't want to die; I just wanted the pain to stop. I wanted to be better. I wanted to recognize myself again.

Therapy has honestly been one of the most painful yet beautiful journeys I've ever embarked on. The very last thing I expected to receive was a mental illness diagnosis. I wasn't prepared for this. Looking back, I realize nothing prepared me for the pain that came in life. Nothing prepared me for heartbreak. Nothing prepared me for my sister Zoie's suicide attempt. Nothing prepared me for Simone's suicide attempt months later. And if you had told me I would need to see a therapist weekly because I tried the same thing, I would have rolled my eyes at you and thought you were losing your mind because suicide feels like such an ugly word.

Like many people, I ignorantly equated suicide with weakness instead of illness. I don't think anyone *chooses* to struggle with suicide. I certainly didn't. I didn't wake up one day and say, "I think I want to be suicidal." The amount of ignorance that surrounds mental illness, in general, is so damaging. This rhetoric is what prolongs people from ever getting the help they need. We must stop talking to people as if they wake up in the morning and choose their battles. We must stop telling people, "It could be worse." Our only job is to love people and point them to Jesus, reminding them there is grace for this. Sometimes that means just listening. Sometimes that means praying. Sometimes that means being there for them.

You can't tell someone struggling with mental illness to be "stronger" because, for most of us, we're fighting with all our strength to be here. And for others, there is not much fight left. Sometimes we don't know why this struggle even happens to us. What I do know, however, is that God's grace is sufficient through it all, and whatever our human minds don't understand, the blood of Jesus covers. In our weakness, He is strong. Every week, I come into my therapist's office grateful for this tool and resource. I've seen God's hand restore me to life.

It has been challenging to feel so exposed and dig down to the root of my issues. I never knew the different ways depression manifested itself in my everyday life. I also had no idea my brain was blocking trauma memories for my protection (more on this later). The chapters ahead chronicle some difficult, ugly experiences. However, I believe we should not have to be quiet about the ugly stuff. I believe God is right in the middle of the ugly stuff, and it is okay to talk about it. So, with that being said, this is a safe space, friend.

If you read Ezekiel 37:1-14, you will see that the "valley of dry bones" I referenced a little bit ago doesn't stay that way. God uses the prophet, Ezekiel, to speak life into those bones, waking them up and giving them air in their lungs. They turn into recognizable people again. They have hope again.

The messiness and brokenness in our lives are constant reminders that there is so much work to complete in us. The beat in our hearts and breath in our lungs indicates that God is not done with that work. And I think if, for nothing else, that's a reason to get up each morning, accept His new mercies drown in His grace, and lean on Him as our Living Hope.

Chapter 2

Nice to Meet You, Jesus

I was about five years old when I thought I knew Jesus. I was born and raised in the church, and my mother and grandmother never let me forget His name. Based on the pictures that I saw, I thought He was a white man with long, flowing hair and a beard. I thought He was someone you should not disobey, or He'd strike you with lightning. He loves to be called Jehovah Jireh. As a five-year-old, I thought that was His middle name. Jesus "Jehovah Jireh" Christ.

I knew He wanted me to be dunked underwater for some reason, and I also knew He wrote a giant book called the Bible that I needed to read in its entirety before I died. I knew He was coming to see me, and I needed to be ready, and I knew to get ready, I needed to be good — whatever that meant for a five-year-old. Last, I knew He loved me and that I could get anything from Him if I was a good girl! I knew Santa Claus wasn't real early on — but Jesus? Jesus was real, and He gave gifts, too.

At eight years old, I sat on my mom's bed and told her I wanted to be saved — whatever that meant for an eight-year-old. I heard a preacher say that I needed to be saved to go to heaven. I knew I didn't want to go to the scary place called hell, so heaven it was.

"Mommy, I want to be saved," I said innocently.

My mother wasn't surprised by my statement because I had to be one of the most mature eight-year-olds on the planet, but I'm sure she knew one day I would fully comprehend what I was saying. Nevertheless, she took my hands and asked me a few questions:

"Do you believe that Jesus died on the cross for your sins? Do you confess with your mouth and believe in your heart that Jesus is Lord?" I shook my head yes to both questions.

"Then you're saved," my mom said. She prayed over me and told me that I was officially a member of God's family. I'm not even going to lie, after that night; I thought I was the coolest third grader on the planet. I walked into school the next day feeling fantastic with my head held high. I was a member of *God's family*.

From then on, I thought I pretty much had it all figured out. I went to middle school, then high school, and I was the "good girl" who never got in any trouble. My mother rarely had to discipline me. I was also known as the "church girl" in school. I thought keeping my grades up, listening to my mom's rules, and being a "good person" would get me into heaven. In retrospect, I unknowingly had a pride issue, and we all know what happens after pride. However, I thought my good work earned gold stars from God. I also thought going to church consistently, following the rules, and singing praise and worship songs automatically put my name in the Book of Life.

In my mind, I was good with God, and God was good with me, but over time, I felt myself just going through the motions.

I sang a hallelujah, gave a praise dance, lifted my hands, and called it "knowing Jesus." Sunday school and choir rehearsal became a routine, and Bible study just became one other thing I had to do. The story of Jonah and the big fish and Noah's ark became recitable stories. It was less about how God showed up in those stories and more about how well I committed them to memory so I could win Bible trivia. I learned quickly that just going through the motions wasn't enough.

When I got to college at 18, riding on my mom and grandma's prayers no longer kept me afloat. Memorizing the story of Jonah and the big fish didn't equip me for spiritual attack, and being able to recite memory verses didn't mean I had a relationship with the Lord. I had been disconnected from the Source of Life for nearly all my life, and I had no idea.

I couldn't understand why resisting temptation in college suddenly became so hard. I was the stereotypical "church girl gone wild." I befriended the wrong people, and the next thing I knew, excessive alcohol was part of my regular activities. I went to parties, got drunk, danced with boys, and thought it was life-giving.

Sin felt much more fulfilling and appealing than reading my Bible. Just like Eve, the devil deceived me into thinking I was "free." I was finally "free" from my mom's rules and the church's regulations. Little did I know, I was more of a slave than ever. When alcohol called my name, I came running. When my ex-boyfriend, Ollie, wanted sex, I came running. When my friends wanted to play dirty games and go to parties, I came running. Sin was my master. Sin dictated my every move like I was a puppet.

It wasn't until Ollie and I broke up that I truly had a wake-up call. I've had many heartbreaks in my life, and each served a different purpose. But the heartbreak from Ollie was what first led me into a real relationship with Jesus. Boy, do I have an insurmountable pile of lessons to share from my relationship with Ollie. But what's a story without a good opening? So, let me set the stage for you.

When I fell in love with Ollie, it happened in three days — no lie. But let's rewind a bit. In my hometown, festivals are a big deal because there's nothing else to do other than eat, go to the mall, or see a movie. One year, as my sisters and I prepared for the local Greek festival, we shopped for new outfits. Finally, the weekend came. Typically, my sisters and I spent the evening together and walked around the festival, exploring and eating, but this year, both my sisters had boyfriends they were meeting up with. However, I was single. So, I walked around alone, having my yearly gyro, fries, and freshly squeezed lemonade.

I sat on a bench to eat and looked around, observing people walking by, which is one of my favorite pastimes. Suddenly, this super attractive guy caught my eye, and I did the whole "sheepish smile and look away" combo. Then, out of the corner of my eye, I saw him walking in my direction. I immediately clammed up, trying to figure out why he would pick the moment I had gyro meat hanging out of my mouth to come and say hello. I quickly tried to wipe away the cucumber sauce from the corners of my mouth with a napkin as he sat down and introduced himself, stretching out his hand for a handshake. I obliged. His name was Ollie. He had the perfect combination of confidence, articulateness, and charm.

Ollie asked me about myself, which was nice. He oddly felt like home to me. There was something so familiar and safe about him. We talked about life for at least 30 minutes, which is uncommon for two strangers. But as I said, he felt safe.

Eventually, he said it was nice to meet me and got up to find his friends with whom he had come to the festival.

Before leaving the bench, Ollie decided it would be better to call his friends first to see where they were instead of walking around the whole festival trying to find them. His phone was dead, though. So, he politely asked to use mine, and I let him. He called his friends, returned my phone, and thanked me. Ollie began to walk away, and I immediately smiled. It felt nice to have a guy listen to me as intently as he did. Suddenly, Ollie turned back around to face me and shyly said,

"So… I have a confession."

"What?" I replied nervously.

"My phone isn't actually dead, and I didn't need to call my friends. I put my number in your contacts; use it if you want…I know you will," he said with a smirk as he walked away.

As I reflect, aside from being a very naïve 19-year-old at the time, I know precisely why Ollie's words charmed me — I've always loved romantic comedies and my life had just turned into one.

I tried to play it off, but I went home with butterflies in my stomach, replaying the whole experience in my head over and over again. "Do I want to call him?" I thought. From the first moment he sat on the bench to talk to me, I *knew* I could love him. It sounds impossible, but I did. Something in me automatically knew that, but later that night, something in me also knew he'd hurt me. You can call it intuition or discernment — either way; I should have listened to it.

At first, I did listen to my gut. I didn't call Ollie. It wasn't just that it didn't feel right, though. I was going back to college, and Ollie didn't live in the same city, so I thought it was pointless to start anything with him anyway. I deleted his phone number and tried to get him out of my head. I wasn't exactly successful at that. I kept thinking about him and how easy the conversation was with him. He felt so familiar.

About three months later, I got a message on Facebook. It was Ollie reaching out to say he hadn't stopped thinking about me. He was surprised I didn't call him. After seeing his message, the butterflies fluttered right back, but I let the message sit there for a few days. I couldn't understand how something could feel both right and wrong. Curiosity eventually got me to respond. I thought maybe—just maybe—the love of my life was waiting on the other side, and all I had to do was message him back. The hopeless romantic in me thought she was opening herself up to the possibility of love.

So, I finally responded, and he asked to see me, but I wasn't ready or even sure about that, so I told him we could text and talk on the phone instead. Even though I turned him down, Ollie relentlessly persisted. No one had ever pursued me like that before. He was eager to see me, and eventually, I agreed. This was mistake number one.

It felt like time froze when we were together. Everything I was supposed to be doing got pushed to the side when he called. Homework was obsolete when he wanted to see me, and nobody else mattered because I just wanted to be with him. I was utterly obsessed, infatuated, and delusional.

Mistake number two was assuming the devil was a scary monster I could point out in the crowd. In reality, the devil disguises himself as our most pleasurable desires because he's a manipulator. Eventually, Ollie and I were exclusive as boyfriend and girlfriend, and the rest of the world didn't matter. Red flags looked green, and we just did our own thing. I didn't know much about accountability at that time, and oh, how I wish I did.

I wore my virginity like a badge of honor — like a prize I won. I ignorantly thought I had special privileges from God because I was a virgin. The church unintentionally taught me that I was different because I hadn't had sex. I looked down on girls who had, feeling as if I was better than them. In retrospect, I felt that way about a lot. Self-righteousness ran thick in my veins.

If we're being honest, very few of us probably learned about sex from the church, not in a healthy way, at least. We were left to figure it out for ourselves, which is a shame because God is the beautiful Creator of it. So, my idea of purity was simply abstinence.

Purity, however, isn't just about abstaining from sex. Purity, like anything else, is about heart posture. It didn't matter that I was a virgin if I struggled with pornography. Watching pornography is just as impure as intercourse. However, for some reason, I was convinced that it wasn't.

Ollie was very intrigued by my virginity. He was shocked that I was a college girl who hadn't had sex. My "badge of honor" became even shinier because of Ollie's intrigue. I defined myself by my virginity and even wore a ring that represented my purity for all the wrong reasons. I felt accomplished and thought I must have been doing something right. If you grew up in "purity culture," you might have had a similar experience. Yet still, fantasies of Ollie permeated my mind, and curiosity came alive in the nighttime hours. Eventually, my self-righteousness came plummeting down. I was soon in the same shoes as the girls I judged.

Often, young women rationalize their actions, even if it's not what they truly want. We tell ourselves, "I'm going to marry him anyway," or "It was just one time." Ollie and I were headed down a path that would soon be extremely difficult for me to escape. With every unconsented touch, persuading word, and captivating glance, Ollie had me exactly where he wanted me.

I finally learned why God intended sex to be between husband and wife. It's a bonding act that should only be created within the covenant and boundaries of marriage. I had an inexplicable connection with Ollie, so when abuse crept in, I excused it. His moods were my moods, and his heart felt like it was beating in my chest. I thought the connection I felt with Ollie meant we would be together forever, so I made excuses for obvious red flags. Our relationship was the entangling of two souls that never made the covenant commitment to be together forever.

After a two-year cycle of sin, Ollie and I ended our relationship. As hard as it was, I just couldn't take the pain anymore. The Ollie I met at the festival was long gone. Generally, the days, weeks, and months leading up to it can be a rollercoaster of emotions when relationships end. I wanted Ollie to fight for our relationship and thought he would. I hoped he would pursue me like he did when we first met. But boy, was I wrong. It was over. I felt so empty inside; it seemed like the last two years of my life had been wasted. I remember feeling completely disillusioned. *"How did I end up here?"* I questioned.

This particular breakup shattered me like never before. I felt like a drinking glass dropped from a five-story building. I lost all my dignity, begging and pleading for him to work it out. Once, I fell to his feet, pleading for him to see my worth as if he were my master. And if I'm being honest, he was. Ollie was my god. Our breakup revealed where my treasure was hidden, and it wasn't with Jesus. I had hidden my treasure with a boy who had no intention of storing it or keeping it safe.

God beckoned over and over for me to give Him my broken

heart. I didn't know how or want to because alcohol bottles were much more appealing. Every night, I drowned myself in liquor and *Grey's Anatomy*. I yearned for the love that the fictional characters had. I cried and screamed, blaming God for my broken heart. I couldn't understand why He would let me continue in a relationship with Ollie if He knew it would end this way. He could see everything, so I couldn't understand why He didn't part the sky to get my attention if He had to. It's funny how our disobedience leads to feelings of entitlement.

This wasn't God's fault. I had free will, and He gave me multiple red flags that I chose to ignore. I mean *multiple.* I ran past each warning with my hands covering my eyes because the relationship with Ollie felt too good. God doesn't force our hands into anything, and I learned that after *falsely* accusing Him, just like the people did at the cross. History really does have a funny way of repeating itself.

Alcohol seemed appealing for some moments but didn't stop the pain, and watching romantic television shows didn't mend my heart. I just felt more and more empty. One night after drinking an entire bottle of alcohol, I was so drunk I urinated on myself because I couldn't stand up to go to the restroom. As I sat in a puddle of my own urine, the Lord asked me if this was what I wanted my life to be like. He said if I wanted to be an alcoholic who masked her pain, I could continue this way. But I had two options: choose alcohol or choose Jesus.

Thankfully, I chose the latter. Choosing Jesus wasn't easy, though. It required me to stop everything I was doing to feel "whole" again. I had to stop obsessing over the lost relationship with Ollie, stop fantasizing about what could have been, stop stalking his social media to see if he had moved on, and stop expecting him to change for me. I had to stop drinking, stop watching romantic shows for the time being, and stop watching pornography. Thankfully, Jesus didn't require all of this at one time. He just wanted my heart.

It wasn't until five months later that I truly understood what it looked like to place my treasure in Jesus. On my 22nd birthday, my friend, Emma, texted the gentlest words to me after I reached out to her, still heartbroken over Ollie.

"You're having a hard time because it was so real for you. You were 100 percent in it for the long haul...It's not wrong to feel everything. Feel it, acknowledge that you feel this way, and then gently place it aside," she texted back.

Oh, how I needed to hear those words. Until then, I didn't realize I had entirely placed my identity in Ollie. That is why it felt like a massive hole had been dug into my heart when he left.

Reluctantly, I finally gave my heart over to the Lord. Honestly, I didn't want Him to have it because I didn't think He could handle my brokenness (go ahead and laugh). Honestly, though, it felt like way too much. I felt so far removed from God and knew it would take some hard work to return. But all He wanted was for me to come home. He promised to take care of the rest.

This breakup catalyzed my relationship with Jesus because it changed everything. It completely changed the way I viewed Christ. It gave me a first-hand look into the heart of the Lord. It led me back to my first true love — Jesus.

After an entire year of intentional healing, I came to fully know God for who He truly was. He wasn't the mean guy in the sky I thought I knew growing up, but my dearest Father and closest Friend. He held me in his arms and rocked me to sleep every night. Every day He said, "Tell me what's wrong," as I cried on my pillow. He reminded me how precious I was. I have never felt that before. I never knew what it felt like to be held in the arms of a loving father.

I had to repeatedly be reminded that my broken view of my identity wasn't accurate. When I felt like I wasn't enough or too hard to love, Jesus gently reminded me that I was meticulously designed by the Creator, who is love. It isn't wrong to want to be loved. We were created as such: to love and be loved. We run into issues, however, when we fail to recognize the difference between flawed human love and the perfect love of Christ. Sometimes we seek love from broken people who can never love us like God. They can never fill the voids like Jesus can.

When I allowed Jesus to be the lover of my soul, I learned that I was so broken and incomplete without Him. I learned that I was not good at protecting my heart or creating healthy boundaries and needed extra accountability. I learned that I struggle with seeking validation from others. I learned that I desperately needed Jesus.

When people experience a bad breakup, it often ruins their outlook on love. But because I took some time to allow the Creator to define love for me, my outlook remained the same — hopeful. And even if romantic love doesn't happen for me here on this earth, I know I've experienced the greatest love there is — the love of Jesus.

You see, love is patient and kind. It does not envy or boast, and it's not rude. It doesn't demand its own way, nor is it irritable. Love doesn't keep a record of wrongs, and it rejoices in the truth. Love never gives up, never loses faith, and it is always hopeful. Lastly, love endures through every circumstance. This is *true* love, not the kind they show you in the movies. And not the kind you think a couple has based on a social media photo.

This is what God says love is. What I experienced with Ollie certainly wasn't love, but it was a painful lesson.

Naturally, we'll mess up and sometimes make the wrong choice regarding love. Sometimes we're blinded by our fleshly desires, thinking that "following our hearts" will lead us to the right person or place. But grace. If grace were an avalanche, we'd be crushed. The Lord knew you and I would need it forever.

Chapter 3

Terrible gods

As I scrolled on Instagram, feelings of abandonment started to creep in. I watched my friends, or who *used* to be my friends, take videos, and make new memories together. One of my worst fears has always been people deciding to leave me, and it felt like that fear just kicked down my door.

During this time, I faced a lot of rejection from people because of an unfortunate situation with my old friend, Emmett. As I consumed my social media feed, I was incredibly hurt because I wasn't invited to celebrate one of our mutual friend's birthdays. My friendship with Emmett had been completely severed, and wherever he went, I couldn't go for the sake of keeping issues and awkwardness at bay. Unfortunately, Emmett was always the one who got included, not me.

A few of my friends decided to go on a road trip to celebrate, and I got left behind. I was doing okay until I saw how much fun everyone had without me. I saw them laughing and enjoying each other's company, which stung. It felt like a crater had been dug into my heart. I couldn't stop crying, and I felt so alone. No one warned me about how painful friendship breakups can be. Being left out reinforced Satan's lie: No one ever cared about me. I couldn't understand how my friends could abandon me like that.

From the very first chapter of this book, I've been open about my attempts at taking my own life, and feeling abandoned is one of the things that always brought me to that low place. This night was no different. I looked at the social media posts and hated that I couldn't be a part of it all. My year felt cursed right from the beginning. I lost my best friend, Emmett, and it felt like I lost everyone else right along with him. I thought dying would be better than the pain I felt at that moment. Again, I asked God why He wouldn't take the pain away. If He knew I was contemplating taking my own life, why would He let the pain continue? Why would he give me friends that were okay with abandoning me?

I tried to force myself to reach out for help because I knew I was beginning to spiral, but I couldn't. I was too embarrassed and ashamed to explain why I felt so sad. "My friends didn't invite me to the party" seemed like a weak reason to kill myself, even though it was much deeper than that. So instead of reaching out to someone to let them know I was in a dark headspace, I just sat there sobbing. I assumed no one would take my call anyway, being how they went on the birthday trip without me. I lay on the floor, cold and crying. I wanted it all to go away. This didn't feel like the God I was happy about in third grade. This didn't feel like the God that gave blessings.

I did not know what else to do other than to sing. I began to rock back and forth and sing worship songs — anything I could think of to ease my mind. And eventually, I fell asleep.

So, how did I get here again? How did I reach the point of

wanting to commit suicide yet again? A friend once told me that people often think your testimony is the story of how you overcame the bad things people did to you, but this is the wrong way of thinking about it. Even though people hurting you may be part of the story, your testimony is what God saved *you* from. What sin were *you* engulfed in? In what ways did *you* harm others? So, with that in mind, the sad story I laid out above, though valid, shifts a bit.

My world was shaken up at the beginning of the year because of my poor actions. I was confronted about an immature lie I told my best friend, Emmett, and I couldn't even begin to explain the embarrassment that followed. Once confronted, my heart immediately dropped into my stomach because I knew I was wrong. This sinful habit had finally caught up with me. In the past, I compulsively lied because I had such a deep identity hole in me that I was unaware of. The fabrications stemmed from my desire to feel loved and valued, so I told extreme lies to get people's "loving" reactions. Emmett wasn't the first person.

I lied to Emmett because I felt like I was beginning to lose my place in his life as his best friend. I wanted to know that I still mattered to him. So, I made up a story about people making fun of me, knowing he'd come to my defense. I knew he'd affirm me, and it always felt good to be affirmed by Emmett. I felt like fainting once he told me that he knew I lied. I wish I could've taken everything back at that moment, but it was too late.

I sat there grappling with how I got to this low place. Why would I tell such a childish lie to my friend just to get a reaction? I had to be honest with myself. I knew I lied because I wanted his love and attention. I felt jealous and insecure because I wasn't confident about my identity in Christ. I immediately felt remorse and wanted to make it right with Emmett. I kept apologizing, but at the time, it wasn't enough. Emmett wanted nothing to do with me. You can't decide how people repair themselves after you've hurt them.

I wish I had more dignity than to grovel and beg someone for forgiveness, though. Don't get me wrong; we are supposed to seek forgiveness, try to reconcile, and make things right when we've wronged someone. However, the begging came from a broken place within me, making me believe my life would be nothing if Emmett weren't in it. So, I tried everything in my power not to lose him. I knew something was seriously wrong with that, and finally, I came to the shocking realization that Emmett was an idol who had replaced God as the king of my heart, just like Ollie did. Once again, I elevated a man over the Man who died for me. I sensed a pattern.

A need for validation was at the root of my friendship with Emmett (and all my close friendships with guys in particular). I felt safe and valued by Emmett. He never failed to make me feel good. His investment in my happiness was a perfect recipe for unhealthy attachment. I tried to fill voids through this friendship that Emmett was never supposed to fill. I became super codependent and didn't know how life would be if I lost the friendship. Before I knew it, I was in a toxic whirlwind of idolatry. Yikes. I didn't recognize this friendship was an idol because it wasn't in the form of a golden statue.

Emmett and I were never more than friends, and we never crossed physical boundaries in any way. My unhealthy attachment to Emmett came from crossing emotional boundaries. I never learned that emotional boundaries were important. I've always been a person who feels like you should not be afraid to pour your heart out to the people you care about. I never learned what "guarding my heart" (Proverbs 4:23) realistically looked like. And I certainly never thought sharing dreams, goals, fears, trauma, past experiences, and other intimate details with a platonic guy friend could be inappropriate or dangerous, but they were.

Kelly Needham's book *Friend*ish was pivotal for me in dealing with this realization. She listed six things that Jesus is supposed to be in our lives: Savior, mediator, shepherd, satisfaction, judge, and boast. It is dangerous when friends become these things for us.

"Idolatrous friendships are not only normative in our culture, they're celebrated as *best* friendship. To the world, a best friend is *supposed to* fill these roles in your life. If two friends can't function without each other, it's not a cause for concern but for celebration that you found your BFF"[1] (*Friend*ish, p. 32).

Kelly hit the nail right on the head. My friendship with Emmett had become idolatrous, and I didn't even know until it came crashing down. I thought having a best friend I relied on for everything was normal. I thought it was normal to tell Emmett everything. I even thought it was normal to expect him to pick me up when I was feeling down and comfort me when I was sad. Not only is this dangerous in any friendship, but it is even more dangerous in an opposite-sex friendship.

After being confronted about the lie I told Emmett, the days that followed were dark. I was isolated and left out of everything I used to be part of. I was called names and gossiped about, and thoughts of suicide overwhelmed me. I felt I did not belong on this earth anymore because I was so ashamed. I thought I deserved the mistreatment because of my poor actions.

---

1   Needham, Kelly. *Friendish*. Nashville, Nelson Books. 2019.

It felt like I had been exiled from my community. And honestly, I was. I was suddenly the "uninvited" girl, which messed with my mind. I went to sleep every night violently shaking from anxiety, and I woke up the next morning feeling the same way. My heart pounded fast, and it felt like I could not control my body.

At first, I blamed God for my pain. It felt like He abandoned me, too. Deep down, I felt a lack of love, and God had nothing to do with it. Though it took me a while to get there, I think I eventually unlocked a new level of understanding. I was reminded that Jesus loves you and me so much that He died knowing there was a possibility that we would never love Him back. And this is where the conviction got real. I did an abysmal job loving Jesus back at this point in my life. I loved people and their opinions more. I looked for their validation and acceptance more. I clung to affirmations from men more. And Jesus took a backseat in my life. That's why I couldn't hear or feel Him. He wasn't far away; my false gods were just in His place.

For a long time, I rode the high of getting my needs met by broken humans, and I felt complete…temporarily. I felt like I had arrived at the happiest point of my life and did not want to hop off the ride. The words of people filled me up, and the words of God became virtually silent.

Then it all came crashing down, as imperfect things do, leaving me in so much pain. I placed much of my identity in people. And guess what? People make terrible gods.

I went to my therapist's office without a clue about how to recover. The name-calling and isolation felt debilitating. People even lied about me throughout the entire situation, but I could not stand up for myself because a lie got me here in the first place, so I felt like no one would believe me. I thought I deserved to be treated like this because I messed up. Words and opinions held a lot of weight at the time. And I had no idea how attached I was to people until it was ripped away, and all I had was Jesus. It felt like even *He* wasn't enough.

Now I realize it was wrong. What I did was wrong, and what they did was equally wrong. This went on for a long time, with ups and downs. I made mistakes, and Emmett said a lot of hurtful words. Most of the time, I just let it happen. He turned into a much different person than the guy I initially befriended. We fought so much that it was exhausting.

I consistently tried my best to reconcile, have mature conversations, smooth things over, and seek mediation, but nothing worked. It honestly hurt so badly. Eventually, I did not even want to be friends with Emmett anymore; I just wanted peace. However, I learned the hard way that humans couldn't be my peace. I pursued reconciliation, but my efforts weren't reciprocated. I felt I deserved apologies I never got, and if I kept waiting around for them, I would have been waiting forever. Furthermore, the bitterness in my heart just kept festering because I was looking for people to make things better for me. So, after a while, it finally hit me that Jesus *alone* had to be my peace.

I went into my closet multiple times a day and just sat at the feet of the Father, feeling so defeated. Most days were ugly cries and screams. I sobbed tirelessly because it felt like I had lost everything. In that closet was the only place I could be my rawest self. I suffered daily, and people had no idea because I had to get back up every time and continue my life as if I wasn't going through so much darkness.

At ministry meetings, I had to sit beside the people who

mistreated me. I had to listen as they planned to eat together after church and not be invited like I used to. The same people who aired out my dirty laundry to others and lied about me were the same people Jesus told me time and time again to love. That kind of strength could only come from the Lord himself.

You would think these people didn't have any sins of their own by how they treated me. As much as I wanted to return their behavior, Jesus nudged me to be kind to them and remember my sin instead. It was so hard, and I didn't do it perfectly. I wanted nothing more than to treat people exactly how they treated me. But God asked me what that would change. How would that help? How would God have gotten the glory out of that? He was doing something more significant and shaping me into a woman with more integrity. He was more concerned about my character.

I lied to Emmett. I can't ignore that fact. I had never been on the receiving end of his anger before, and it wasn't pretty. You can't control how people retaliate, but you must remember that your worth and identity cannot come from someone who did not create you. So even though his pain and feelings were valid, they did not determine my worth or value. I was sorry, remorseful, and making changes. That is all I could do.

After acknowledging and apologizing for my wrongs, there was nothing else I could do to salvage this friendship, but for some reason, I kept trying to force Emmett to see how sorry I was and why he should forgive me. The reality is this; we are not entitled to anyone's forgiveness. As God's children, we are expected to forgive others, but not everyone lives by that. When I think about it, I wanted Emmett's forgiveness more than God's. I knew God would forgive me, but what about Emmett? I wanted to make sure he did too. I could not bear the thought of losing him.

I realized I was begging Emmett for forgiveness before I even thought about repenting to God. This let me know where my treasure was truly stored. I allowed my friendship with Emmett to replace Jesus on the throne of my heart, and it came crashing down instantly. Again, people make terrible gods.

As I explored this with my therapist, Ava, she explained that it was normal for people with PTSD to struggle with codependency and identity issues. At first, it was off-putting to hear because sometimes it is hard to hear such brutal truths about ourselves. But she was right. I had no idea who I was. So, when someone who cared about me came along, it was easy to get wrapped up in them and lose myself. I accepted the labels that others placed on me. It was easy to ingest those words and make them my new truths. My self-esteem plummeted, and I thought killing myself would be better than feeling like this. I plotted ways to do it, but again the Lord stepped in as my refuge.

You would think after all the hurt, pain, and revelations of idolatry that came from my issues with Emmett; I would shift some things, however; when it comes to this silly heart of mine, I tend to be the kind of person who must fall on her face about three times before I finally get it right.

Emmett and I eventually made up and brushed over what the real issue was. We had a mediated session with our pastor that seemed to work for a little while. We knew our friendship had to shift a bit, but no one guided us on what that would look like. We had little birds in our ears here and there, but I don't think either of us completely understood the severity of our unhealthy attachment.

Once we became friends again, we picked right back up

exactly where we left off. It felt normal and comfortable for a short time. Then, the arguments trickled back in, and issues popped back up. We couldn't figure out what the problem was. Even after realizing this friendship had become an idol, it felt like I was too entangled to let it go. And with zero accountability in my life, I was able to tell half-truths and lie to myself that things were better.

Finally, the truth came to light for me. Jesus was never the foundation of my and Emmett's friendship. We built our friendship on each other's empty voids. Emmett's struggle with male friendships and my struggle with female friendships was the perfect storm for an unhealthy connection.

The bottom line was that I did not truly believe God was enough for me. I had a lot of head knowledge about Him being my everything — my protector, my provider, my true love, my healer, and my daily bread; however, I had such a hard time moving those promises from my head to my heart. I had an easier time believing people, especially men, were my everything. My perception of God was flawed.

In hindsight, my relationship with my parents significantly affected my desperate desire for love and validation. Because I came from a broken home, I gave my heart away without hesitation, hoping to get love in return.

I wanted to give every part of my soul away to a guy because I thought that was what I was supposed to do. I loved hard, boundaries never existed, and I wanted the guys in my life to get everything I had to offer. I gave away lump sums of money, made outlandish purchases for guys, denied my personal needs to make them feel comfortable, and allowed guys to manipulate and walk all over me. The brokenness was two-fold, though. Not only did I allow myself to be abused, I also abused others. I lied and manipulated often. I wanted to be loved so badly, and I said anything to get it.

It all came full circle one night after personal worship and prayer time. I opened one of my notebooks and found notes from an online Bible study I had been doing. I looked at the bottom of the page and read something I drew a box around. It said:

"One way to know God's voice — He shines a light on the ailment of your soul before He addresses the issues in your life."

I was *utterly floored.* In other words, often, we want God to make things better. Most of us hate suffering and want it to be eased instantly. Our human nature elevates comfort and pleasure above all else. Anything we want is at our fingertips. Lonely? Download a dating app that gives you access to thousands of people ready to fill that void. Need to know an answer? Google it. Tired of someone in your life? Cut them off. Hate your job? Quit. For the most part, we do not have to work hard for anything, nor do we have to wait for long periods of time to get it.

God doesn't work that way. He works on His own time, which is always for our good and His glory. So, this note in my journal hits on a crucial point. Though I wanted God to remove my pain, He had other plans that required me to trust Him. Most times, God does not just take our pain away. He is waiting for us to invite Him into it so He can press into the root of our issues. But first, I had to stop lying and trying to manipulate the outcome. I had to stop hiding.

He wanted to meet me in those trenches, but it was my job to bare my soul, be honest, and invite Him down there. We cannot heal what we continue to hide. When I did invite Him into my mess, it wasn't pretty. But He definitely makes beauty out of ashes.

Chapter 4

99 Problems and Identity is 1

Every present struggle has an origin story — usually from childhood experiences. And at the root of every struggle is sin which also has an origin story: Adam and Eve. How much do you want to bet that the forbidden fruit they ate didn't even taste that good? Or maybe it was to die for, literally. Either way, I know it wasn't worth bringing sin into the world. Since then, we've been trading righteous favor for rotten fruit, and it shows.

Emptiness followed me in every season of my life. I struggled with feeling like I wasn't important or special to anyone. I called myself worthless and every other negative word I could mutter. I couldn't pinpoint exactly what was wrong, but I knew I didn't love myself and longed for someone who did. I looked through old journals and read entries that repeatedly chronicled the same issues. I consistently wrote about not having anyone who cared about me or loved me over the years.

Night after night, I pitied myself. I felt as though no one could ever possibly love me as the mess I was, and night after night, Jesus raised His hand to let me know that He already did, but I overlooked it. My cries were too loud, and my pain was too great. I was so tired of suffering from brokenness. The hurtful words of past relationships and friendships constantly echoed in my brain. Maybe I was too clingy or cried too much. Perhaps I was too sassy, and no one wanted to deal with me. Maybe I wasn't exciting enough or spontaneous enough, or pretty enough. These were the thoughts that invaded my mind.

As a result of this broken perception of myself, I constantly sought validation from guys. I liked to be around guys who gave me a lot of attention. Compliments from boys made me feel outstanding, and with my love language being words of affirmation, I clung to every compliment any boy ever gave me. This started at a very young age.

"Can Jordyn come out and play?" Levi used to ask my mom.

We were five years old and lived right next door to each other. Levi was my first friend. We played outside almost every day and explored nature together (as much as we could in our driveways where our parents could see us). Levi was there for many of my first memories. He rooted me on as I learned to ride my bike without training wheels, he watched the dances I choreographed for fun and even joined in sometimes, he helped my mom patch things up when I fell off my bike and scraped my leg, and as we grew older, he was always there to advise about the boys I liked. We were rock solid.

Starting at five years old, I've had a lot of male best friends. That is all I had in high school and through college. Each one held a different place in my heart and made me feel important. They always told me I was smart, pretty, a good person, and deserved the world. One even called me an "angel" once and said he hoped I got everything I wanted in life. It made me feel so good. I never had a big brother (but always wanted one), so my male friends filled that role for me.

I know I also looked for my dad in every single one of them because even though I know my dad, I didn't grow up with him in my home, nor did I ever get affirmations or advice about guys from him. He wasn't very involved in my life, so my male friends pretty much filled the roles I wish a big brother and my dad had filled. I felt no one would ever harm me around my guy friends. I felt cared for and protected.

I've always struggled with the scripture on "guarding your heart" (Proverbs 4:23) because I've always been a hopeless romantic. Give me a rom-com, chicken wings, and a Friday night, and I am seriously in my happy place, with or without someone sitting next to me. There is just something about the storyline of romantic comedies that never ceases to make my heart do cartwheels.

Boy meets girl, they feel instant chemistry and fall in love; either boy or girl is not ready for the relationship or messes things up, they go their separate ways (but not really) and then somehow end up crossing paths again and realizing what a mistake they made, and then they ride off into the sunset together. You can always predict the storyline, but it still gets me every single time.

However, romantic comedies had honestly created so much discord in my personal life, especially when I wasn't mature enough to filter fiction from real life. There is always a disconnect between the movie plot and my reality. The movies don't consider the real damage that comes from heartbreak. These movies leave out the part where you may have to go to therapy for some time because your expectations of love are utterly shattered, and you no longer know who you are. These movies leave out the scene that shows how two broken people will never complete each other no matter how hard they try.

The desire for love and adoration was at the root of all my friendships with guys, even though I disguised it as platonic friendship. I prided myself on being "just friends" with guys. It was too late when I realized I was in love with my friend, Emmett, from the last chapter. My heart was already invested, and before I knew it, I was in a whirlwind of emotions that were so hard to keep in check.

It happened quickly. We had so much in common, from music and television shows to creative and intellectual commonalities. We did nearly everything together. It is rare to find someone who has almost identical interests as you, and also alarming. At first, I didn't know I had romantic feelings developing. I just thought I was blessed enough to find the greatest best friend ever. It felt surreal.

I remember how Emmett seemed to care about me so much more than I had ever experienced from a person. He would check on me and see how I was doing almost every day; we texted all day, every day, we talked on the phone and video called when we could, and we hung out every chance we got. Emmett would ask if I had eaten and brought food to my house; he paid for and pumped my gas and surprised me with concert tickets. Whenever I mentioned liking or wanting something, he surprised me with it about a week later, and he always invested in my creative endeavors. It was like a dream come true.

"God, what did I do to deserve a friend like this?" I asked.

The same was true for me. Once I learned Emmett's love language was receiving gifts, I tried to flood him with gifts every chance I got. I paid attention to what he pointed out at stores and would go back and buy it for him too. I spent much more money on Emmett than I would like to admit. I helped with whatever I could in his creative and business endeavors, and I was always there to encourage and build him up whenever he was down. After a while, I started to tilt my head sideways with curiosity because it almost seemed like we were much more than friends.

Cue the romance movie.

I began to imagine how amazing it would be to end up marrying my best friend, and that's when I realized, at the very least, I was attracted to him. Emmett knew precisely what to do and say to make me feel special, important, and valued. Soon I acknowledged that it wasn't just attraction I felt, but I was starting to fall for Emmett, and it was both exhilarating and confusing.

I wasn't sure if I should express my feelings to him because I feared messing up the friendship we had cultivated. However, I knew keeping it to myself would drive me crazy because I would never know if he felt the same way. From where I was sitting, his actions surely indicated he did, but I needed to hear him say it. After two hours of going back and forth about whether I should express my feelings for Emmett one night, I finally mustered up the courage to tell him.

I figured we had built a strong enough friendship foundation to withstand the awkwardness of any unreciprocated feelings. At the time, I felt like I was honestly invested in the friendship alone — anything more would have been icing on the cake, but I convinced myself that I was also okay with staying platonic. Emmett's friendship meant a lot to me, and I couldn't see it going away. Either he liked me, or he did not feel the same way. I knew it would not change how great of a friend I thought he was, nor did I want to stop being friends if the feelings were unreciprocated.

One night, I sent him a text message that was as straightforward as possible. I wanted to know if he had feelings for me and followed up with examples of his actions that indicated he might like me, too. It didn't take long for him to respond. When I saw the three iMessage dots pop up showing that he was typing, my heart began to race because I honestly wasn't sure what he would say. I remember the message like it was yesterday.

Emmett: Jordyn, I love being around you, and I love being your friend. We literally have so much in common, but I don't think I have any feelings for you other than friendship.

Me: Okay, thank you!

I felt embarrassed responding that way, but it was all I could think of. I didn't expect to cry that night, but I did. I was sure I would be okay no matter Emmett's response. But I felt a little embarrassed for laying my heart on the line. I also felt confused by him. Baffled.

Why did he do everything he did for me if he did not like me as more than a friend? I couldn't quite understand but feared that asking those questions would create tension between us that I didn't want. So, I dropped it. I told myself I was invested solely in the friendship and could get over my feelings while remaining friends with him. Needless to say, honey, I was wrong.

Emmett shared his deepest hurts about past friendships and trauma as our friendship grew, and I felt like I needed to place my romantic feelings aside and show up for him as a good friend. I told myself that my feelings didn't matter. In my head, Emmett needed someone to take care of him and show him that genuine friendships do exist. I fully convinced myself that I was the person to take on that role. I felt like I needed to be his protector. I thought he *needed* me to be his friend because life was already hard enough for him. I thought it would be selfish to pull away so I could get past my romantic feelings for him when he needed friendship the most. Plus, I loved being his friend. So, I did what I thought was best at the time — I remained his friend.

That being said, I assumed Emmett would adjust his actions so they would not be "misunderstood" again, but he did not change one thing. He still bought me everything I wanted and brought food to my house when I was hungry. He still talked to me all day, every day, and he still invited me to hang out with him all the time. He still affirmed me and made me feel special. He still went out of his way to make sure I was happy. Everything remained the same, and it really confused me, but it also felt incredibly good. I felt loved, cherished, and noticed. So still, I remained quiet. I tried my best to be a good friend to him.

When I realized the romantic feelings weren't going away, I expressed to Emmett that I thought we should probably take some time apart so I could get a handle on things. My heart was full-on doing backflips at this point. So, we decided to limit communication and stop hanging out one-on-one, but it only lasted maybe a week because we both gravitated back to each other. So, we went on as usual.

I look back and realize how much we played with fire. I knew our "friendship" was something I needed to let go of for a while, but I didn't speak up. I was afraid of losing Emmett. I was afraid that I wouldn't feel special anymore. So, we continued to do life together. People asked about us and wondered if we were dating, but we laughed it off. However, it honestly affected me. When other people thought we would make a "cute couple," my heart jumped a little. It bred a glimmer of hope that maybe Emmett would eventually agree with them.

Then things shifted. There was one night I'll never forget. I went on a trip to Indiana with some friends, and we were at a birthday party. My friend Dakota and I were sitting around talking, and she asked me how my date with Emmett went.

"Huh?" I responded in a puzzled tone.

She told me that Emmett said he had asked me on a date, and she wanted to know how it went. I was super confused because I understood that Emmett did not like me romantically, so why would he tell someone we were going on a date?

This new information could only mean a couple of things: either Emmett did have feelings for me but was afraid to tell me, or Emmett was taking advantage of my feelings for him and playing me like a fool behind my back. Any way you spin it, I was a mess. I didn't know how to feel but knew I needed to talk to Emmett.

I was open about my feelings and just wanted to know the truth. Emmett denied ever saying he took me out on a date. I knew in my heart that I didn't believe him, but all I could do was ask for his honesty. I asked, and he answered, so against my gut feeling, I left it alone.

This went on for about two years. During those years, I suppressed my feelings, telling myself I was okay and didn't need time apart from Emmett. Though the friendship with Emmett started very satisfying, it didn't stay that way. At first, we were best friends, and it was great. We knew everything about each other, knew the traumas that shaped us, and knew each other's mannerisms and facial expressions to a science. It felt so good to be seen and heard.

We revisited the conversation about romantic feelings at least once more, but nothing changed. I wasn't strong enough to set proper boundaries, and he didn't think they were necessary. So, I continued to push the feelings down deeper, and little did I know, I was soon going to crack. And I did.

As I sat in a therapy session crying to Ava, she said, "So it sounds like you have identity issues, which is pretty common in codependent people."

"Ummm, excuse me?" I thought. Me? Codependent? Identity issues?

I was sitting there heartbroken, and this is her conclusion? What about Emmett? Why didn't she say anything about his actions? It rubbed me the wrong way, to say the least, and I stewed on it the whole drive home. I ranted to God, called my therapist weird, and thought about never returning to therapy. But then God fed me a piece of humble pie and revealed why she was right.

I often found myself in "situationships" and friendships with guys who loved parts of me but only the parts that benefited them. It felt good to be wanted. I was super broken with identity issues but was getting the desired attention, so I overlooked the warning signs that I was becoming extremely codependent with Emmett. I missed his red flags, too. I felt valuable because guys would give me words of affirmation, seek advice, use my creativity, or want to spend time with me.

I placed my identity in what I could offer men, but it left me feeling so broken when they no longer wanted me. One particular instance with Emmett landed me in the hospital after another suicide attempt. That is how deep the identity hole was.

Only through my mistakes and God's grace can I sit here and write about the dangers of codependency. God is a healer, and

His love covers a multitude of sins. I can honestly say it is so much better on the other side — the side of deliverance.

There are a lot of moving parts to codependency. It was first only used to describe the partners, friends, and family members of alcoholics. The term has since expanded and describes a condition that affects a person's ability to have healthy and mutually satisfying relationships. There is such a mental, emotional, physical, and/or spiritual reliance on another person that you can't function independently anymore. The other person defines your mood, identity, and happiness. Codependency can affect any relationship, including children, parents, friends, romantic partners, siblings, co-workers, etc.

Researchers studied the relationships of people with alcohol addictions. They found that codependency is a learned behavior, usually during childhood, when the dependent person witnesses family members who also have codependent behaviors. People who battle codependency often think their needs are not important because they are often disregarded, so instead, the person shifts their attention to someone who is addicted or ill because the needy person relies on them and makes them feel wanted and desired.

I grew up in a household where my feelings were often dismissed. I was raised in a single-parent home, and my mother had to be the breadwinner to provide for my sisters and me, so emotional needs went unmet. Because my innate need for attention and affection was unmet, I sought relationships to meet those needs.

I discovered what a beast codependency was when my friendship with Emmett inevitably came crashing down. I felt confused, lost, and heartbroken. I couldn't understand how something I invested so much in could be gone in the blink of an eye. Relationships, even friendships, created through codependency often turn abusive, one-sided, or emotionally destructive. Unfortunately, I thought Emmett and I were good for each other, so I never anticipated it turning so sour.

Chapter 5

Just Friends

My friend, Marshall, tried to warn me. He told me to pull back a little because as he observed my friendship with Emmett, he was worried I would spiral. He told me it wasn't realistic to remain friends with someone while having romantic feelings for them. And deep down, I think I knew he was right, but at that time, I laughed it off because I hoped he was just being over-analytical. As our mutual friend, Marshall watched everything unfold right before his eyes exactly how he predicted it would.

Marshall and I sat down for coffee one day, and he described my and Emmett's friendship as the "perfect storm," but I didn't listen. I grew increasingly codependent on Emmett. Marshall told me he could see the dopamine release in my brain whenever Emmett walked into the room. He said he watched me turn into a completely different person, and my mood switched instantly when I was around Emmett. Marshall knew I was in love with Emmett before I even knew I was. What Marshall said to me planted a seed, though.

I started to notice little differences in my behavior that my friend Marshall tried to warn me about. I felt jealous of any woman Emmett spoke to or hung out with. I couldn't stop imagining us as a couple because it felt like we were. On the inside, I was suffering because I was best friends with someone who made me feel special like I was their girlfriend, but I had no valid claim to him whatsoever. He could do whatever he wanted, hang out with whomever he wanted, talk to whomever he wanted, and I was never allowed to have an opinion about it because he wasn't my boyfriend. But my heart slowly broke little by little.

Has anyone else ever been in a situation like this before? A "situationship"? A situationship can most easily be defined as an undefined relationship with someone. You say you're not together, but it doesn't look that way. It's more than a friendship, but it technically isn't romantic either. It's a connection with someone where the lines are often blurred, and emotional intimacy goes far beyond a platonic friendship.

As I mentioned in the last chapter, Emmett never failed to make me feel special. I won't lie; I enjoyed the attention. But because this situation with Emmett remained unresolved and lacked proper boundaries, it didn't play out in my favor and turned abusive. Emmett would make me feel so special and showered me with gifts and favors one day (i.e., love bombing), and then he would completely shut down and give me the silent treatment the next day (i.e., stonewalling). It did not go well when I confronted Emmett about what I noticed.

It's common for individuals to get defensive when confronted about their harmful actions. This results in lying, gaslighting, or even turning it around on the other person. They may shift blame and project. I often found myself apologizing even when I didn't do anything wrong. I constantly second-guessed my gut instincts and ended up feeling like I was the issue. It started to affect me mentally and emotionally. I felt like I was losing my mind.

I was so attached to Emmett that I would lie and manipulate him back to feel his love again (i.e., trauma bonding). Unfortunately, this only gave him leverage to assassinate my character. It became very easy to get all our friends on his side by telling them about all the "unhinged things" I was doing. And this just made me more desperate to get the "loving" Emmett back. It was a twisted and sinful cycle that led to more emptiness. I searched for validation in someone who could never give me everything I needed because no human can.

It's common for codependent people to also suffer from mental illness or addiction. Codependency isn't a diagnosis alone; it is often just a symptom. Having PTSD, clinical depression, and anxiety make me more prone to codependent behaviors and identity issues. So, when my therapist told me I had identity issues, she was right. I'm grateful she called it out. Without this knowledge and God's grace, I don't know if I would have recovered from the deep end. But I did.

I've seen a lot of healing in this area. Sometimes I see codependency trying to creep into my relationships, particularly when conflict arises. My instinct is to hold on for dear life if I feel like I'm being rejected, pushed away, or abandoned. And I tend to overextend myself to prove I'm worth being in someone's life. This is all rooted in identity issues.

When I feel this way, I must be cautious and remind myself that the only relationship my identity is tied to is my relationship with Jesus. The Bible tells us that even though we must face suffering and trials here on earth, we can be sure that every detail of our life is worked into something good for those who love God (Romans 8:18, 28).

If you struggle with codependency and find yourself in abusive situations, it's time to seek help. I know first-hand what it's like to lose yourself in a relationship with someone else, whether it's romantic, professional, familial, or a friendship. I know what it's like to be beaten down by someone you thought would protect you. I know what it's like to be taken advantage of by someone you trusted. And I know what it's like to silence your voice because the perks of being quiet feel safer than advocacy.

Though I'm not a doctor, psychologist, or licensed professional counselor, I want to give you a few signs of codependency:

- Low self-esteem
- Poor boundaries with others
- A need for control
- Obsessions
- Lying
- An extreme need for approval or recognition
- Walking on eggshells and avoiding conflict
- Feeling sorry even when they hurt you
- Putting people on pedestals

Please note that there are other signs and symptoms, so this is not an exhaustive list.

I could go on and on about the things I felt Emmett did wrong and could have done differently, but playing the blame game would be of no benefit because I'm sure if you ask Emmett, he has a much different story, with many different motives for his actions during our friendship.

The moment Emmett told me that he didn't feel the same way about me, I should have told him that he needed to adjust his actions to match his words. Even though he said he wasn't interested in pursuing more, it didn't feel that way. I became emotionally attached because of the closeness of our relationship — anyone would. Secondly, I should have given myself the space to grieve the unreciprocated feelings that hurt much worse than anticipated. I deserved that. I deserved the time to heal, put up boundaries, and have them be respected.

If we were truly friends with a good foundation, then we should have been able to come back together and be platonic friends with emotional boundaries in place. Proper emotional boundaries should have been in place from the beginning so we could both be more responsible about guarding our hearts, time, and attention.

In my humble opinion, there's no logical reason a platonic guy friend should be surprising you with gifts and treating you like the most important woman in his life if he has no intentions of pursuing a committed relationship with you. Period. And this is no shots fired at Emmett or any other guy who may have done or is doing this, but rather wisdom. It is very unwise to blur the lines between platonic and romantic relationships. It can get messy very quickly. As brothers and sisters in Christ, we should be concerned about each other's hearts.

I believe we have a responsibility to each other to be very clear, honest, and intentional with our actions. If someone is confusing in any way, you're allowed to call that behavior out. Though it may be a little awkward and uncomfortable, you have every right to ask questions, seek clarity, and ask that specific actions stop. Don't feel bad if someone gets upset with you for wanting to set a boundary to protect your heart. That's on

51

them, not you.

Furthermore, we should always be accountable to someone so relationships don't lead to abuse. We're horrendous at keeping ourselves in check 24/7. Even though I went to my Pastor at the time about these issues I was having with Emmett, nothing truly changed. There was a massive emphasis on behavior modification instead of heart transformation. Temporarily changing behavior doesn't get to the root of sin, though. You must surrender in humility and completely turn away from the sin, sincerely apologize to those you've hurt, ask for their forgiveness, and make things right (Matthew 5:23-24).

Sadly, Emmett and I never got to have this tough conversation. He refused to listen to me about this, and he hated the idea of getting our Pastor involved. I was unable to share my hurt and experiences with him. At the very least, I thought our friendship would leave room for that, but it didn't. I sincerely apologized and confessed to Emmett for what I contributed to the chaos, but I never received that in return. This is sometimes how the cookie crumbles.

As dramatic as it sounds, I used to think this situation with Emmett was the bane of my existence. I couldn't understand how a great friendship turned this sour so quickly. But the Lord reminded me that this wasn't just a sudden downfall. Every small decision, lack of a decision, lack of a boundary, abuse tactic, and pursuit of sinful pleasure was like pumping air into the fire. No wonder it finally combusted. But grace. The Lord is a teacher, and your mistakes don't ever have to be the end. He brings dead things to life.

Ask me now if men and women can be "just friends," my answer has changed a bit. Yes, I do think they can be just friends — with boundaries. There should be a clear difference in how platonic friends interact versus how a boyfriend and girlfriend interact. Furthermore, you must always check in with yourself and be honest about your affection. If something changes your feelings towards a friend, you should pray about it and communicate it. And if the other person's words and actions become confusing, you should address it. This is simply the wisest and most responsible thing to do to protect yourself and others.

However, saying men and women can't be friends leads to an extremely unsatisfying life. Both men and women, made in God's image, offer something uniquely different and beautiful that reveals the nature and character of God. When men and women relate to each other as they were designed to, these relationships can bring so much joy.

Not every man or woman you meet is supposed to be considered a potential spouse. I have male friends who are some of the most remarkable Christian men on this earth, and they also behave like my brothers. I can count on them to offer a wise male perspective. But we all have boundaries in place for our friendships. That is what keeps them safe and honorable.

I believe friendship with people of both sexes is something to cherish. When we begin to think we can't be friends with the opposite sex, we not only deny ourselves the joy that both men and women bring to the table, but we stunt the development of our social skills. It's important to know how to be friends with people of the opposite sex without expecting it to turn into something more. That's just way too much pressure and a very unrealistic expectation.

That said, I don't believe it is wise for men and women to be **best friends.** If someone of the opposite sex is your "go-to" person for everything, including emotional release, I think you're treading on dangerous ground, and there is always a risk for one or both people developing romantic feelings. Sharing intimate details and consistently confiding in one another is dangerous and, I'd even say, inappropriate. Creating that kind of environment is unfair if you don't plan on fostering it through long-term commitment.

The level of commitment in a relationship should determine the level of emotional intimacy and the amount of "access" that person has to you. Emmett and I shared way too much for a platonic friendship. I gave him access to parts of my heart that should have been reserved for the man God has for me.

I think it's also worth mentioning that for those of you who desire marriage, you can honor your future spouse before you get married in many ways. We can honor a future spouse and even ourselves by making sure we are intentional with how we direct our affections. I placed Emmett in the space of my heart that honestly should have been reserved for someone who chose to be with me.

Someone who hasn't committed to you shouldn't have as much access to your heart. It can be dangerous when you allow yourself to be so vulnerable with someone before it is time. The Bible warns us of this. "Promise me, O women of Jerusalem, by the gazelles and wild deer, not to awaken love until the time is right" (Song of Songs 2:7). Protecting our hearts, having proper boundaries, and being honest with ourselves and others, not only keeps us from "awakening" love before its time but also keeps us from awakening love with the wrong person.

Furthermore, non-marriage relationships that mimic marriage are wrong, no matter what society tries to tell us. No, it's not cute to have a work spouse. And no, your friends should not occupy a spousal role as you "wait." There's a time and place for deep emotional connection, and I don't believe your platonic friendship with the opposite sex is that place. It just leads to confusion, unmet expectations, and heartbreak.

As generations progress, we tend to love connection but hate commitment. That's what makes "situationships" so easy to fall into. You can't convince me that Emmett didn't like how I made him feel, even if he didn't intend for it to be more than friendship. He enjoyed the attention. He enjoyed the praise. He enjoyed the gifts and the compliments. He enjoyed feeling special. Who wouldn't?

I think he had emotional voids I filled for him just like he did for me. My heart was wholly invested in someone without a plan to reciprocate that investment. And honestly, he wasn't required to. Emmett was not obligated to feel the same way about me, but I think he was responsible for being more careful once he knew that's how I felt. We both were. My purpose for discussing this isn't to harbor on this situation with Emmett but to be honest and hopefully encourage others like us.

We were two broken people who found more comfort in each other than in Jesus. We both had an emptiness that we transferred to each other because we weren't careful about guarding our hearts. We were selfish in getting our needs met, and it turned unhealthy. We shared details we shouldn't have, creating this exclusivity between us that others couldn't kick down to offer wisdom or accountability, which was a huge red flag.

Whenever you feel others are not welcome into your "friend-ship," you have probably crossed the platonic friendship line. Exclusive and possessive friendships are not only unhealthy, but they are also sinful. This is true for all friendships. No one "belongs" to us.

Do I think Emmett went into our friendship plotting to hurt me? No, I truly don't. And I certainly didn't plan to hurt him. Most of the time, we're all just searching for love in the wrong places. Emmett, if you're reading this, you know exactly who you are, and I forgive you. I pray that you also forgive me.

Chapter 6

More Precious Than Rubies

Until my late-20's, I could only count the number of female friends I've had on one hand. *"I just get along with guys better,"* I always told myself whenever I had a conflict with a girl. I felt like girls didn't like me. We always got into conflicts, and I couldn't bond with them. I didn't enjoy their company and wanted nothing to do with them. Plus, I always had so many guy friends around that it didn't bother me that I wasn't having any luck with female friends.

I used to scoff at people who claimed guys and girls couldn't "just be friends" because I had a long list of names that proved we could. I prided myself on being able to befriend guys and maintain the friendship without romantic feelings ever being involved. In high school, my friend, Adrianna, told me that I had a lot of guy friends because I was a "flirt." Her words offended me.

Am I a flirt? I thought to myself.

Pridefully, the answer was a hard no, although I should have considered what Adrianna said a possibility. At the time, I felt I just meshed better with guys than with girls. This was my experience for a couple of decades. I never thought to do some soul-searching on why I enjoyed and cherished my friendships with guys more than the ones I had with girls.

In my experience, girls were catty, full of drama, and always jealous. I had no desire ever to be a part of it. My friendships with women never lasted. In my mind, *they* were always the problem. So, this pattern of only having guy friends continued for two decades. At every school, grade, and season, I was always the kind of girl with close guy friends, and I preferred it that way.

One day, as I was reading commentary to a passage of scripture, I came across a note about how issues with people are a good indicator that we have issues in our relationship with God. Spoiler alert: Making friends with women wasn't the problem; I was. When things ended up crashing and burning with Emmett, it led me to the gut-wrenching realization that I desperately needed a community of women.

After the heartbreaking experience of not only losing Emmett as a friend but also the heartbreak of unrequited love, I looked around for the support of women to love me through that pain and realized I neglected all of them. I finally had to face this serious problem. Something had to break in my current patterns for me to see the toxicity of them.

Want to know the ugly truth? I secretly preferred friendship with guys because they made me feel good about myself, as we've gathered through the last couple of chapters. I loved the attention coming from guys. Furthermore, girls felt like a threat to my self-worth. I felt very uncomfortable around them. I had so many insecurities that I covered up with the phrase, "I just get along with guys better."

I was addicted to the way affirmations from guys made me

feel. It was like they had something to offer that women couldn't. I didn't see the value of friendship with women because I thought they couldn't offer me much. Women brought the same thing I brought to the table, so what did I need them for?

But everything is rooted in something.

As a child, a female family member molested me. One year, when that family member visited me, the forgotten trauma suddenly flooded back along with a full-blown panic attack. Though I plan to go into more detail about this abuse in a later chapter, I mention it now because therapy taught me that trauma shaped how I consciously and subconsciously felt about women. From a very early age, my mind and body learned that women and their touch were unsafe. So, on the surface, it felt like I just got along with guys better, but deep down, I was that little, abused girl who needed healing.

A friend once told me that if you don't deal with your past, it will undoubtedly come back and deal with you. Whether we like it or not, our past shapes us. It directly affects our emotional, physical, spiritual, and mental well-being.

For a long time, I sought validation from guys without knowing why. Being a lover of words of affirmation became unhealthy because I began relying on those affirmations from men to feel good about myself. And when I didn't get them, I'd figure out a way to get it — lying, manipulation, thirst trapping, and whatever other forms of brokenness I could use to feel loved. I shared every intimate detail about myself with men to seem unique and intriguing. I used to give my heart over to any guy that would take it in hopes of feeling loved.

These were the broken parts of myself that I didn't talk about with anyone because they seemed too ugly. But that's precisely what the devil wants us to do, right? He wants us to be quiet and keep falling into perpetual secret sin. He tricks us into thinking we're okay if no one knows about it. But friends, I'm here to call the devil what he is –– a liar.

Little did I know, recklessly giving parts of myself away to guys would create unhealthy emotional bonds with many of them. This led to serious sin that consisted of ugly cycles of codependency, sexual immorality, idols, and a desperation for love I would do anything to get. I was so broken and lost, it felt like pieces of me were scattered everywhere, and I was beyond repair.

But grace.

Through grace and therapy, I have had to work to rewire my brain about how healthy friendships should look. I've failed a lot, but I've also experienced many victories. As I write, this is the first season of my life where I have not had a male "best friend," and it's…*different*. I'm still learning how to be in this space and accept God's grace for it. One huge win is that I now recognize the utter importance of a community of women surrounding me.

I've had the amazing opportunity to get close to one group of women, and I can't even begin to describe the amount of healing that has taken place. One girl sent me this text message below that completely wrecked me. She said:

Hey sis! I've been thinking about you and just wanted to encourage you. I know you're going through a tough time with friendships right now, but I just wanted to let you know that who you are and your worth isn't based on what happened. Regardless of all that went down, you have people that want to be in your life and want you in theirs! I am one of those people. I always have such a great time being around you, and I am looking forward to hanging out more. I am excited to be a part of your life!

I was completely wrong about women having nothing to offer me because, during one of the lowest times of my life, it was a sister who came in and loved me so tremendously with her kind words. It was a sister who rubbed my back during brunch and let me know that it was okay not to be okay. It was a sister who would pick up my phone calls at 2 a.m. when my thoughts felt like too much to handle. And it was a sister who intentionally included me in plans and ensured I no longer kept isolating myself in my house after my situation with Emmett, hiding all that God created me to be.

When people hear me speak about my new revelation about the importance of same-sex friendships, they assume I am anti-opposite-sex friendships, but this is untrue. As mentioned in the previous chapter, I believe men and women can be friends if they remain honest in communication and healthy boundaries exist.

I genuinely believe both men and women have unique God-given qualities that bring joy in life, and we should respect and cherish those differences. We were all created so beautifully in the image of God. However, my personal issue was being addicted to friendship with men and neglecting friendship with women. I know many others with the same story.

I wholeheartedly believe that having more friendships with women could have prevented a lot of heartache and mistakes. I'm sure someone would have grabbed me by the collar and pointed me away from a path of destruction. A woman could have lovingly held me accountable when I was deep in sin. A woman could have even recognized and brought attention to my brokenness because she shared the same brokenness.

The support of sisters can help us through some of the most challenging times in life. We don't have to walk alone. Women can understand how each other feels in ways some men cannot. A sense of camaraderie comes with being able to fall completely limp and broken in the arms of a sister who gets it. I'm much stronger and experienced so much love and support during that vulnerable time in my life because I finally gave it a chance. I finally allowed God to work on my heart and open up to the possibility that maybe, just maybe, a sister in Christ could love me in the way I needed to be loved.

I feel so emotional writing about this because it's been such a long journey, y'all. I didn't realize how much healing awaited me on the other side of my friendships with women. Furthermore, I didn't know how much my heart and soul needed and even *desired* it. Solely having friendships with men temporarily filled the voids in my heart that only Jesus could fill. I believe having healthy friendships with Godly women, however, would have pointed me to Jesus as my source of healing.

To the girl who prefers guy friends and only seeks friendships with them, I challenge you to ask yourself why. Ask yourself why you put more energy into relationships with men than your sisters. Be honest with yourself about why you prefer the company of men instead of women. Ask yourself the hard questions: Are women always jealous of me? Or am I jealous of them? Are women difficult, or am I just bad at conflict resolution, and friendships with guys is the easy way out?

There are always reasons for our preferences that are probably much deeper rooted in brokenness than we think. Seek healing for those areas. Though I know God is our ultimate healer, I also believe He uses relationships with others to cultivate that healing. I'm a living witness to that. When I fell flat on my face, it wasn't validation from a man that picked me up; it was the healing love of sisterhood.

I don't get this "sisterhood" thing perfect every time. Sometimes I struggle because I'm still learning how to be friends with women. Retraining my brain to believe that women are safe has been a journey that requires intentional decision-making. When I don't feel like answering one of their calls, I answer it anyway. When I feel uncomfortable with one of them rubbing my back to comfort me, I decide to let it happen anyway. When we butt heads, and I want to cut them off (like I did before), I engage in healthy dialogue and work through the issues instead. Every day I must decide to *fight for* my friendships with women. It has made all the difference.

This newness in my life has also required some other intentional decision-making. A couple of guys have shown interest in me on social media, which usually leads to private messages from them seeking to "be my friend." Am I saying this is necessarily bad? No. However, I turned them down and expressed that I'm focusing on building friendships with women this season.

The old me would have cringed at the thought of doing that because I was afraid that I would miss an opportunity to meet the love of my life. But I had to choose — either hang out with those guys or continue to be intentional with the women in my life. Guys can be a serious distraction for me, so to be honest about that, I chose the women. There is not an ounce in me that doesn't believe God won't honor that. I don't believe I could have "missed out" on my husband because of those decisions. There is no way in the world you can be in the will of God and miss His blessings, even if they come a little later than expected. I decided to focus my attention on intentional friendship with women over fleeting validation from men, and that's something to be proud of.

63

This means so much to me because I have had a prayer on my prayer board for over six years that says, "Make and maintain more female friends," and I watched God answer that prayer. All it took was my "yes." I've learned that positioning yourself and opening yourself up for the answer to the prayer is just as important as the prayer itself. And the Lord has proven Himself to be faithful. But I mean — can we expect anything less?

I've watched some of my female friends find love and witnessed their journeys from dating to marriage. It's so exciting to see. I've had my times of feeling discouraged in this area and feeling like this experience with Emmett was a setback I could have avoided. I used to think I was too broken for anyone to choose me and plagued with always choosing the wrong guy. Jesus constantly reminds me that He has already chosen me and loves me unconditionally. So, I've been enjoying my singleness. I've been working hard on deepening my relationship with Christ.

My single life has been an example that there is more cake than wedding cake. From our earliest years, society and the church groom women to think that marriage is the ultimate goal, and though marriage is a beautiful thing and I still desire it, God never promised us marriage. So, to tell people that life isn't complete unless you get married leads them to disappointment. There's more to life than being a wife; I've spent years discovering that.

I started writing letters to my future husband as an exercise for myself to remind me that it is okay to desire marriage and pray for what you want. The letters are less about my desire for the man (whoever he is) and more about praying about his character. I don't want a man who isn't kind to me. I don't want a man who doesn't appreciate me. I don't want a man who abuses me. So, I've been praying for qualities like God-fearing, kindness, selflessness, and gentleness because these mean a lot to me. Furthermore, I've been praying that I become that woman.

I used to feel so much shame about falling in love with Emmett. I beat myself up for a long time because I felt like a statistic –– just another girl who fell in love with her guy best friend. I wasn't exempt after all. But please take it from me; there is absolutely nothing to be ashamed of, my sweet friends. All guilt and shame died with Jesus on the cross. We were created by a God who is love, so it's not surprising that love is so important to us. We want to love and be loved, and that's a God-given, holy desire. The way we seek it, however, does matter.

I have since stopped calling myself criticizing for loving Emmett and changed the way I speak to myself. I've decided to be more kind to myself. I deserve love; in fact, I am already so loved by friends, family, and most importantly, the Creator of the universe. I'm glad I can love something other than myself. I am hopeful that someday, I'll meet a man who wants nothing more than to love me the way Christ loves the church. And now I know I'll have a community of women around me that will never let me forget that it's worth the wait.

Chapter 7

Seventy Times Seven

528. FIVE. HUNDRED. TWENTY. EIGHT. The number echoed loud as I stared at the computer screen, hoping it was a mistake. Just a couple of months ago, my credit score was 708, and now it's 528. *"How could someone do this?"* I asked myself with tears in my eyes. This unwise favor for a friend went terribly wrong, and the effects were catastrophic. When I confronted the friend about these lies that ruined my credit, everything fell apart.

I wrestled with the idea of forgiveness. I knew all the scriptures about forgiveness, but this seemed too hard. This was my financial future we were talking about. I worked hard to build good credit, and it came tumbling down after I went on a limb to help someone I thought was a good friend. So, forgiveness almost felt like a smack in the face. It was hard for me to understand why God required this from me. It felt like God was asking me to overlook everything.

The hard truth is this; forgiveness is a decision we're asked to make with or without answers, with or without apologies, and with or without remorse from the other person. Hear me when I say that it's not easy, and it certainly doesn't mean that what happened to you was right or fair.

One night, I was driving home from worship rehearsal, having a panic attack. I had an elevated heart rate, was breathing heavily, and felt like my mind and body were disconnected. I felt the tension in my shoulders and abdomen, making driving hard.

One can be triggered instantly, seeing someone or hearing their voice. A whirlwind of emotions can flood your body. When I saw this friend that night, my mind flashed back to all the hurtful words that had been said to me, all the hurtful things that had been done, and even though I thought I had forgiven, my flesh wanted everyone else to know the wrong. But the Holy Spirit told me that exposing wrongs in that way wasn't the answer. So, I exploded on the way home. The anger, bitterness, and hurt I had harbored in my heart finally spilled out immediately, leading to a mental breakdown.

I got in the shower and let the cold water run over me. Showering in cold water is a technique I learned to cope with anxiety. It helps bring my mind back to reality. So, I sat in the shower for about an hour and sobbed until I couldn't anymore. This was the first time I had consciously ever experienced the physical effects of unforgiveness. I heard a quote before that says, "Unforgiveness is like drinking a cup of poison and expecting the other person to get sick." I understood this quote in a very real way that night.

For the next few days, I isolated myself. I went to work, came home, and didn't fulfill any of my other responsibilities because I couldn't. I felt debilitated. In retrospect, I just needed the time and space to be honest with the Lord about my hurt feelings. He welcomed me to do that. In the name of "positivity," I had been lying to myself for months, thinking I had truly forgiven when all I did was shove it all down because I felt like I had to. I thought that's what a "good Christian" should do. I never allowed God to invade my heart because I wasn't honest with Him about my hurt about this. I didn't want to make the people around me uncomfortable, so I faked forgiveness so people wouldn't call me bitter.

Spoiler alert: you can't fake forgiveness. Eventually, the mess in your heart comes to light. So, I allowed myself to just *feel* for a few days. I was brutally honest with God and myself because it was time to process and truly work through the suppressed hurt and anger. This wasn't a perfect process, and it still isn't, but it's necessary.

In Matthew chapter 18, Peter asked Jesus how often he should forgive someone who sins against him. I imagine Peter, like many of us, may have been trying to find a loophole. He probably wanted to know how many times he had to forgive someone before he was justified in *not* forgiving them. The scriptures don't tell us the reason Peter asked. Maybe a particular person kept wronging Peter, and he wanted to know why he had to keep forgiving them.

Peter sounds a lot like me. I've asked this question before. "Lord, how many times do I have to forgive them? They keep committing the same offense." Much like Peter, I wanted to know the maximum for forgiveness. Seven times? Eight times? Then can I tell them off? Then am I justified in harboring negative feelings toward them?

"No, not seven times," Jesus replied, "but seventy times seven!" In other words, forgiveness doesn't have a ceiling. And to tell you the truth, I'm still reconciling with this.

At one point in time, I'm sure we've all held a grudge or have been very slow to forgive if we forgive at all. As followers of Jesus, it is Christ's instruction that we forgive, love, be kindhearted and patient, but truthfully, these can be very difficult to do when a person has wronged us.

I used to question why I should be the one to quickly forgive when the other person is the one who wronged me. Mark 11:25 gave me the answer: *"And when you stand praying, if you hold anything against anyone, forgive them, so that your Father in heaven may forgive you your sins."*

This scripture reminded me I have no right to hold grudges and operate in unforgiveness. When we accept Jesus as our Lord and Savior, we will experience a lifetime of forgiveness from God that we don't deserve, so who are we to harbor unforgiveness against others?

I know my feelings were valid. But I could only focus on the pain of the betrayal. I was heartbroken. God revealed a lesson about putting humans on pedestals. I learned never to place someone so high that they can't mess up because they will. People mess up all the time, including you and me. But if I'm being honest, I didn't like this revelation or lesson. So, I kept looking for scriptures that would agree with me.

I continued to flip the pages of my Bible aggressively and landed on a passage in Matthew about revenge:

You have heard the law that says the punishment must match the injury: An eye for an eye, and a tooth for a tooth. But I say, do not resist an evil person! If someone slaps you on the right cheek, offer the other cheek also. If you are sued in court and your shirt is taken from you, give your coat, too. If a soldier demands that you carry his gear for a mile, carry it two miles. Give to those who ask, and don't turn away from those who want to borrow (Matthew 5:38-42).

If I can be honest, this passage upset me instantly. I cried out to God in confusion, wondering why on earth I would let someone slap me and then turn the other cheek for them to hit me again. It was counterintuitive, especially in a culture that calls for you to "do people how they do you" and "match their energy."

Our culture glorifies cutting people off and treating them exactly how they treat you, but the Bible calls us to operate differently. It tells us to bless the people who hurt us and love those who hate us. The passage of Scripture didn't sit right with me, but I know the Scripture wasn't the issue — my heart was. So, I decided to seek understanding. I asked the Lord to reveal what this passage of Scripture meant. Soon after, the Holy Spirit spoke to me gently.

You see, it's easy for us to call out each other's flaws and keep a record of wrongdoing. What if God treated us this way? We'd never, ever be back in good standing with Him. And I know what you might be thinking. We aren't God, so we don't have the same capacity to forgive. But how is it that we consider ourselves more deserving of grace just because we didn't mess up this time? How is it that we immediately desire forgiveness from God and others when we do wrong but can't extend that forgiveness to people when we're wronged? The Holy Spirit was trying to show me that I slap God in the face all the time when I sin, yet He loves me relentlessly. I hurt Him over and over, yet He never leaves. I grieve His Spirit, yet it's still inside me. I ask for more stuff, despite having all that I need. I take from Him without thinking twice about it. Sometimes I even think I've *earned* something — as if I've ever done anything to deserve His grace, mercy, or favor.

Corinthians 13:5 brings up an interesting point to think about when we consider the act of forgiveness. It talks about how love does not keep a record of wrongs. Jesus is our perfect example of this. He paid the price for our sins on the cross and kept no record of the sins we committed. Instead, He asked God to forgive us. His compassion led Him to pray for us.

Many people think this passage means that if you remember a past offense or are still hurt about it, you must be harboring unforgiveness in your heart, but that's not true. Even when you decide to forgive, your heart may take a while to heal.

The problem, however, is when we hold these hurt feelings and memories *against* people, which affects how we treat them. I do not believe this scripture is telling us to let people continue to mistreat or abuse us, but rather handle conflict biblically (Matthew 18: 15-17), do all you can to seek peace (Romans 12:18), and operate in a spirit of humility, knowing that God will fight every single one of our battles (Exodus 14:14).

I want to clarify that forgiveness is not a free pass for people to harm you. Healthy boundaries are godly. God asks us to be good stewards of what He has given us, including our time, money, gifts, and hearts. Therefore, forgiveness is a change in the posture of your heart, not a reason to allow people to stomp all over it.

For example, if someone is verbally abusive and doesn't have respect when they speak to you, a boundary is necessary for the protection of your peace as well as your personhood. So, maybe that looks like only conversing with the person when other people are around. This allows you to love the person still while protecting yourself as an image-bearer of Christ. The fact that God made us in His image is enough reason ALONE to deserve and treat others with respect.

Note the difference between a wall and a boundary, though. Harboring unforgiveness in our hearts puts up a wall. I don't believe we're supposed to put walls up against people because walls keep others out altogether. I don't believe we can truly operate in love — both receiving and giving it — if we have a wall up to keep people out. Boundaries are more flexible. Depending on the situation and the person, they can be readjusted or even eventually removed. They don't block people out of your life; instead, they are just a safeguard that determines the level of access someone can have to you. Boundaries still allow room for you to love others and others to love you. They still allow room for grace and forgiveness.

Forgiveness is a muscle we, as followers of Christ, get to strengthen. I know from personal experience that can be difficult. Forgiveness didn't happen overnight when I worked through heartbreak, trying to forgive the friend who ruined my credit. I woke up each day feeling anger, hurt, and bitterness. My struggle wasn't a sign that I wasn't reaching complete forgiveness, though. It was merely a sign that I was human and that something still needed to be mended. So, you know what I did? I allowed myself to feel that anger, hurt, and bitterness every day, and then I laid it down at the feet of the Father. I had to do that repeatedly until healing occurred and I could forgive and truly let go. Healing is rarely a one-time occurrence but rather an ongoing process. As long as we're here on this earth, we'll always be working on this because people are imperfect and mess up just like we do. Are you willing to continue the race, knowing that the God of the Universe is leading it?

I want to encourage those who may be struggling with forgiving others. You are not alone. My therapist once told me that if I wait for a person's apology to move on, I could be waiting forever. Furthermore, Jesus never told us we should only forgive if the other person apologizes. He simply said to forgive over and over again. But what if this was his gracious gift to us? What if, in His all-knowing power, God is aware that our fragile human hearts cannot bear the cancer of bitterness and unforgiveness? Forgiveness helps soften the heart, and it's like therapy for the soul.

We often hold a grudge against people because we think that's how we get justice and punish them. It's a way we keep people indebted to us and stay in control. But this isn't true. If you don't think forgiveness is necessary, consider how you feel when the person who hurt you comes to mind. Do you feel at peace? I can bet you don't. Bitterness disrupts your well-being, mental health, and emotional health. The longer you refuse to forgive someone, the longer they have power over you. By keeping a record of wrongs, you're choosing to hold onto the very thing that has robbed your peace.

It is not our job to nail someone to the cross for sins Jesus already died for, but there is a reason Jesus tells us to love and forgive. There's always a reason. We may never fully understand, but I am a living witness that forgiveness set me free, both when God forgave me and when I forgive others.

Chapter 8

P.S. I Love You

Whenever I need a reminder of my growth, I pull out the old journals I've kept over the years. I like to read about what I used to desire or what I used to struggle with. One night, I came across something that I wrote called *Grace for the Broken Hearted*.

To the people who feel so misunderstood they don't even talk anymore, I hear you.

It feels like you're going in circles with others, trying to get them to understand why you're hurting, but they're on a mission to misunderstand and misinterpret every word you say.

*To the people who try to open up only to be met with answers from others suggesting **you're** the problem, I hear you. Most times, you just want a listening ear, yet they have the answers you weren't even looking for, so your venting session turns into a blame fest, and somehow, they've become the victim.*

To the people who spend countless nights crying alone in debilitating anxiety because you don't know when the next time you'll feel okay again, I hear you. Your pillow soaks up your tears, and you sit in a cold shower feeling numb, but at least you know you're alive.

To the people who crave human connection and weren't prepared for the loneliness of adulthood, I hear you. You want to spend quality time with others, but you don't want to feel like a chore, so you try to cling to God instead, but He seems so silent. You're making an honest attempt to fill your Jesus-shaped voids, but He seems so far away.

To the people who are misunderstood, ignored, rejected, lonely, anxious, and just plain broken-hearted, I hear you. I am you.

But there's grace for us, too.

As you can probably tell, I was hurting and confused. I was lonely. But I could acknowledge that God's grace was enough despite my heart breaking. I haven't always been able to recognize God's grace. I've struggled to believe that in my weakness, He is strong.

One night, I kept thinking about all my failed friendships and the unkind words that plagued my heart. I couldn't understand how worthlessness made itself at home in my life. I kept asking all the "why" questions. Why am I the one who got abandoned by friends? Why do they get to be happy? Why do they get to experience a full life, and I don't? Why did they get away with treating me poorly? Why do I have to be in so much pain? Why doesn't anyone care about me or love me?

All the lies, negativity, and comparison got louder and louder, and it felt like I couldn't control my thoughts. I allowed them to control me instead. I felt empty and worthless and decided I didn't want to feel the pain anymore. It felt like God was so distant and just watching me hurt. I began to get angry with Him. Why was He watching me break like this? I wanted Him to say *something* that indicated He cared about me. I was looking for a sign, a picture, a quote, something to let me know He saw my pain. But that moment never came. Well, I'm guessing He probably did, but I was just too engulfed in my thoughts and emotions to notice.

I wrote a note to my friends and family saying that I was sorry that I wasn't strong enough to fight this pain and sorry for the hurt I was going to cause by ending my life. I took many pills and lay there waiting for them to kick in. After about 45 minutes, I felt stomach pain and got nervous, but I continued to lay there because the devil had such a firm grip on my mind. He led me to believe that I wanted to die.

After about 2 hours, the stomach pain started to increase, and I kept jumping out of my sleep with a racing heart, sweating profusely. I kept going to the bathroom. On one of the bathroom trips, I felt so grieved that I was doing this. I tried to force myself to throw up the pills, but it didn't work. Again, the devil led me to believe this must be my fate. I remember unlocking the top lock of my apartment door in case someone had to kick it down to come to get me. I went back to bed and closed my eyes. I knew there was a good chance this could go two different ways. I would either pass away in my sleep or wake up in the morning. It's clear which one ended up happening.

When I woke up the next morning, I felt no better emotionally, mentally, or physically. I texted my friend, Dakota, to tell her what I had tried to do. She was shocked and called me right away.

"I'm glad you were honest with me, but now I have to do something, Jordyn. I can't keep letting you do this," Dakota said. She seemed so frustrated with me. This was the third suicide attempt, so I'm sure she was afraid. Dakota wanted me to get help. Though I was in therapy regularly, sometimes you need extra help. I didn't believe that at the time, but now I know that on some days and seasons, we struggle more than usual or we struggle differently. Dakota asked me to go to the hospital and get myself committed.

"I'd call and have you committed myself, but you're over 18," Dakota said.

She annoyed me with that statement, and I wished I hadn't told her. But deep down, I knew she was right. At that moment, I needed a little extra help mentally, and that was okay. But it didn't *feel* okay. Not one bit. This is the part about struggling with suicide that I hate — people wanting you committed, the horrible hospital stays, the constant questions. It's so embarrassing. But I followed through.

I went to the emergency room and told them everything. I wasn't sure of the physical ramifications of my actions and needed a medical professional to help me if there was any damage. Different people kept coming into my hospital room asking me the same questions:

Did you do this on purpose?

Tell me about what's going on.

How many pills did you take?

What kind of pills did you take?

I wanted help, but this was starting to annoy me. I know they were doing their jobs, but I was utterly humiliated by why I was there. I was still in a dark headspace and secretly wished the suicide attempt had worked; then, I wouldn't have to go through this embarrassing part.

The nurses took my blood, checked my heart, and then I had to wait for the results. I watched workers pass by, saw people in masks because of the COVID-19 pandemic, and heard doctors and nurses laughing. The funny thing is, being in this hospital during a global pandemic was the calmest I had felt in years.

My blood work and exams came back clean. I didn't ingest enough to do physical damage. I wish I could say I was grateful to hear the good news, but I wasn't. I felt like a failure. I had just put myself through all this embarrassment for no reason.

After talking to a psychiatrist, the doctor decided I could go home. They said because I see a therapist regularly and would start taking supplements to help with my depression, then I have the right resources to help with my mental health. If I promised not to harm myself again, I could go home. Even though I didn't know him, the nurse said he cared about me and wanted me to live. I wish I could say I believed him. He made me promise I wouldn't try it again. I felt so uneasy making a promise I didn't know I could keep.

I was sad for a few days. The depression didn't lift right away. I knew God wanted me to come to Him, but I didn't know how. I didn't feel like praying, worshiping, or reading my Bible. I didn't feel like talking to people about what happened. I didn't feel like resisting the devil so he would flee. I didn't feel like "thinking happy thoughts." The only thing I felt like doing was lying in my sorrow. I still didn't see the value of my life for the next few days, but I was alive for a reason.

The thing is, God wasn't asking me to feel less sad. He wasn't even asking me to be grateful that I was still alive. He simply asked me to let Him lay there with me. I realized that I had to permit myself to *grieve.* There's so much weight to that word. Sometimes society invalidates our grief. If it isn't a personal loss, like the death of a close friend or family member, then people tell us that our sadness is invalid. That's just not true. I had a lot to be sad about. I lost myself and lost friendships. I needed to grieve.

I listened to a podcast episode that was very healing for me. The host spoke about giving ourselves the space and time to grieve in a culture that puts a time limit on sadness. Jobs offer one week of grievance before you need to go back to work. Some friends offer only so much support, then get tired of holding you up. But grief is complicated, and it seldom goes as planned, which is why sometimes people can grieve for 10-plus years.

God doesn't turn a blind eye to our sorrow, so why should we? We can't plan our pain, but one beautiful and powerful thing I've learned is that we can invite the Lord into our pain. He feels with us. He cries with us. He has been in our shoes. There's one quote from Carrie Lloyd, who was the guest on the podcast episode, that I will never forget:

"I love redemption stories, but if we don't look at the grief, we don't know where the Lord is going to show up."

I love this quote so much because, too often, we try to breeze past our pain. Like Paul, we pray that God removes the thorn in our side. But God says, "No, I want to do something with that thorn." God is waiting for us to invite Him into our pain. He wants us to talk about it with Him, feel through it with Him, and heal through it with Him. The moments I've experienced the fullness of God are the moments I was hurting beyond measure. He continuously places His nail-pierced hands on my aching soul, and I've never felt a love like that anywhere else.

Now that I am looking back, there were so many signs that I wanted to live that day, but the devil kept lying to me, and I kept believing it. The fact that I was even sitting in that hospital bed showed that I cared at least enough to get help. And that's worth a lot. Those decisions mean so much, friends.

If you are someone who struggles with feeling worthless, I understand. I've been there so many times and still must fight off that lie. It hasn't been perfect, but I think that is the reason we need a perfect Savior. I've struggled with depression since I was a teenager. And in almost every season of my life, I return to Psalm 42. Read this with me:

1 As the deer longs for streams of water, so I long for you, O God. 2 I thirst for God, the living God. When can I go and stand before him? 3 Day and night I have only tears for food, while my enemies continually taunt me, saying, "Where is this God of yours?" 4 My heart is breaking as I remember how it used to be: I walked among the crowds of worshipers, leading a great procession to the house of God, singing for joy and giving thanks amid the sound of a great celebration! 5 Why am I discouraged? Why is my heart so sad? I will put my hope in God! I will praise him again — my Savior and 6 my God! Now I am deeply discouraged, but I will remember you — even from distant Mount Hermon, the source of the Jordan, from the land of Mount Mizar. 7 I hear the tumult of the raging seas as your waves and surging tides sweep over me. 8 But each day the LORD pours his unfailing love upon me, and through each night I sing his songs, praying to God who gives me life. 9 "O God my rock," I cry, "Why have you forgotten me? Why must I wander around in grief, oppressed by my enemies?" 10 Their taunts break my bones. They scoff, "Where is this God of yours?" 11 Why am I discouraged? Why is my heart so sad? I will put my hope in God! I will praise him again — my Savior and my God! (Psalm 42).

Verse one is one of my favorite scriptures of all time, but the entire passage encourages me because it lets me know that it is okay to have those wavering moments of faith when things don't look so great. The passage reminds me to remain honest with the Lord and let Him know my afflictions. Even in moments of depression, I know that I can still praise and worship God. Depression and worship are not mutually exclusive. We can be sad and bow down at the feet of the Father at the same time. In fact, He invites it.

R.C. Sproul once said, "I don't always feel His presence. But God's promises do not depend upon my feelings; they rest upon His integrity." Dear friends, accept this today. Our feelings are valid but skewed. They often do not reflect complete truth but what we perceive as true. For that very reason, we must believe in the integrity and character of God. He keeps His promises. He is exactly who He says He is, and that doesn't change based on our feelings. He is everything we're not and then some. Because of Jesus' blood on the cross, depression doesn't win in the end.

I used to think my struggle with mental illness would be the end of me. I honestly didn't think I would make it past 25 years old. But because Jesus died on the cross for us, we have hope that life won't be like this forever. It was never meant to be a life of pain, illness, or heartbreak. When you accept Jesus Christ as your Lord and Savior, your eternity will look much different. There will be no more sadness, mental illness, bitterness, pain, or heartache. And we get to experience a glimpse of that eternity now.

Even if things look bleak now, I promise there's another side! I promise God is with you. Today, I'm writing from a place of healing; praise God! I have recently been able to stop taking antidepressants and manage my mental health more holistically. Therapy and medication allowed me to learn effective methods for managing mental illness. I am now three years free of suicidal thoughts and attempts and no longer need the antidepressants. God can do more than we could ever imagine.

Medication was a tool from the Lord. Without taking something to help with the chemistry of my brain, I wouldn't have been healed enough to wean off of it. Jesus was more than enough to heal the imbalances in my brain; medication was simply the tool He used to keep me living so that I could experience that healing.

Some people won't agree with that, but oh well. I stopped caring what other people thought about how I should handle my mental health a long time ago. I could no longer afford to be weighed down with opinions about this. It was quite literally about life or death.

Though we may struggle in this lifetime, this life is only temporary when you put your faith in Christ. One day, because of the blood shed for us, we get to live eternally with God in heaven, where there will be no more brokenness. All feelings of worthlessness will cease to exist. Christ defeated it all, and in Him, we have hope. If you can believe and hold on tight to that — you, my sweet friend, are living out the essence of the Gospel.

Chapter 9

Shattered Souls, Part 1

Sage has always been a brave girl. She is vocal about her thoughts and is unafraid to challenge anyone. When she called me on my lunch break one day, I thought it was to tell me about a conflict she had gotten into with someone. I remember answering the FaceTime call in complete shock. She was just beaten.

Sage had gotten into a heated argument with her husband in the car. He then grabbed her hair, wrapped it around his hand, and slammed her head off the dashboard. Her daughter was in the back seat. They pulled over to the side of the road, and Sage was forced to get out of the car.

She stumbled across a golf course in broad daylight, trying to find help. I answered the video call only to see Sage's bloody, beaten face. Her forehead was gashed open, and her lips were swollen and bloody. I told her she needed to hang up with me and call the police for help immediately. I called one of our mutual friends who went to get Sage and take her to the hospital. Thank God there was no severe physical damage. However, the emotional damage was catastrophic. Sage was heartbroken, disillusioned, and angry. Before 20 years old, Sage had already experienced so much trauma. Unfortunately, Sage wasn't "new" to abuse. She was sexually abused before as a young teenage girl.

"I told my dad, but he never did anything," Sage muttered after revealing she was sexually assaulted by someone she knew when she was about 14. It had been over eight years since then, but the memory came to her as if it happened yesterday.

Sage never expected to be a victim of sexual abuse — no one does. Sage was coined "promiscuous" and blamed for what he did to her. People told her she had "no business being around all those boys." No one saw her as a victim, and because of that, she didn't speak up about it again for nearly a decade.

Someone who should have been a protector took advantage of her. He saw a weak, innocent girl, and he preyed on her. Other people knew, and no one said anything. Even her own father knew and ignored her. Someone should have advocated for her. How come no one advocated for her?

I wish I could say this is rare, but it's not. The reported abuse numbers are staggering, and some victims still can't tell their stories. Emotional, verbal, physical, and sexual abuse are injected deep inside their veins, hidden like a bruised rib under a shirt. It happens much more often than we talk about.

One day, Sage called me. She was concerned that her daughter's daycare had hired a new male employee. I know Sage's worry came from her own experiences with abuse, so she was naturally protective of her daughter. I validated her concerns, but it also made me think about how many males are overlooked in the conversation on abuse. The stigma that boys "don't get abused" couldn't be any further from the truth. Women can be abusers, too.

I know guys who lost their virginity to older women at 13 and 14 years old and think it's a badge of honor. There is nothing honorable about this. Those women were predators with attraction to children. It's not an honor; it's evil. Some communities have created a false narrative that a teenage boy who loses his virginity to an older woman is now a "man," but he's not. He's a victim.

I know far too many quiet households on this subject, and the devil is having a field day with it. The only way to overcome darkness is to shine it under the light of God's holiness. Call this evilness out for what it is: sickly demonic.

I wish I knew then what I know now because my story is no different than Sage's. Quite frankly, I thought abuse was something that happened to other people. I didn't think it would ever happen to me until it came knocking on my front door.

I believe that my ex-boyfriend, Ollie, never intended to hear the word "no." I was 19 years old when I met him. Remember the charming guy I met at the Greek festival? He made me think he respected my decision to save sex for marriage. Early on, he knew my faith, values, and convictions. They *intrigued* Ollie. In retrospect, I honestly believe my virginity intrigued him because he saw it as a game. He wanted to see how quickly he could get me to change my mind about purity.

One day, Ollie and I were hanging out, sitting in my car as always, enjoying each other's company. We weren't in an official relationship at this point, but we liked each other. If I'm being honest, I loved him already. I spent every night I was able to with Ollie. This particular night, we were in the car talking about what we wanted to do with life. It was the first time we had this conversation, and I loved it. I told him about my dream of becoming a New York Times best-selling author but that I was currently in college, taking the easy way out. I picked Speech Pathology as my major because I knew I would make good money and that the field needed more people who "looked like me." But honestly, I was miserable.

"Why don't you write, then?" Ollie asked.

I told him that I do write and love to write, but I didn't know if I could make a career out of it. Ollie nodded along, but I could tell he wasn't listening to me anymore. I asked Ollie about himself. He wanted to become one of the nation's most renowned sports agents. He played football but didn't see playing it as a career. He was more passionate about the business side of things. I think his ability to talk about his vision with such clarity is what sucked me in. I've always had a thing for articulate guys.

Ollie was soon no longer interested in discussing dreams and goals but kissing instead. *"Is this what I want?"* I questioned internally. I knew the answer was no. I clearly articulated my boundaries, so why did I feel like they meant nothing? Why didn't my "no" mean anything? I was conflicted between feeling uncomfortable and in love, so I just let it continue. It is difficult to remove yourself from a situation when you love someone, even when it turns unhealthy. The night quickly turned into one that would be so hard to heal from.

My body froze up, and I sat there feeling lifeless. My mood quickly turned to anger and rage, and I felt a hatred for Ollie welling up inside of me. I kicked him out of my car and told him never to speak to me again. I cried driving the entire way home, blaming myself because I didn't move his hand. I was mortified.

I remember Ollie calling me 17 times in a row that night,

and I ignored every single one. But then I saw a voicemail notification. I should have ignored that, too. As I listened, my heart grew soft from the shakiness of his voice and his crying.

"I'm so sorry, Jordyn. I never meant to hurt you. I love you," Ollie sobbed. That was the first time he had ever said he loved me. His apologies sounded sincere, but I needed time to think.

Enter Satan. He saw that I was weak, confused, and vulnerable and preyed on that. Satan knew exactly how to lure me. After this incident with Ollie, my sexual senses heightened. Satan used Ollie to plant a seed in me that grew into curiosity. I thought about my sexuality in a way I never had before and was confused by the mixed feelings. I watched pornography to try to understand what was happening to me.

On the one hand, I knew sexual immorality was sinful, but on the other hand, Ollie's "I love you" kept echoing in my head. I wish I had talked to someone about what I was experiencing and my family had discussed sex more openly in my home. Open dialogue would have provided a more well-rounded sexual ethic — a healthy one.

One day, curiosity got the best of me, and I started researching sex. I came across an article written by a Christian woman. She wrote about why she regretted waiting until marriage to have sex. She wrote angrily about how her local church shamed her for wanting to explore her body. She was scared into wearing a purity ring and remaining abstinent. This teaching led to utter disappointment on her wedding night because she felt ashamed of her body and had no idea how to express her sexuality.

Thinking about this now, she was right about one thing: The Church should not have shamed her for being curious about her sexuality. God created sexuality, and it is beautiful. She should have been able to ask questions and have a healthy dialogue.

Someone should have explained why God designed sex for marriage instead of scaring her into keeping her virginity. If the Church presented sex more healthily, I don't think she would have walked out of her marriage suite on her honeymoon night feeling defeated and ashamed.

Reading this article and my experience with Ollie watered the sinful seed planted inside of me. I agreed with this woman's sentiments and didn't even know her. However, I was also raised in the church and never had a healthy view of sex. The church taught me three things about sex: it's bad, don't do it, and you'll get pregnant. I thought my purity ring would guard against the filthy forces surrounding me. Spoiler alert: it didn't. I got to the end of that article feeling like the church lied to me about sex too, but it wasn't enough to forgive Ollie immediately. What he did was still wrong.

After about a week, I finally returned Ollie's calls. I listened to what he had to say and felt awful for ignoring him. Once we rekindled, Ollie told me he was upset with me for "making him feel weak." He hated that he called me so many times with no response and that he cried over me, crushing his pride. He told me he hated me for that. He made himself the victim even though he was the opposite. This is called blame-shifting. I wish I had all the knowledge that I have now. He would not have been able to get away with this, but at the time, he did, and I found myself apologizing to *him.*

Ollie and I quickly made up. I was sucked back in by his false promises. Under the guise of "love," I looked past the sexual abuse that occurred from that night a week ago and dove headfirst into an official relationship with him. I told myself I must have been important to him if he wanted to make it official.

For about two years, we went on having our ups and downs. When it was good, it was *really* good. But the bad would leave me feeling crushed. We would break up, then get back together again, then break up, then get back together again, just in cycles. There was always this gut feeling that something was off, which I now know was the Holy Spirit. The Lord constantly gave me gentle nudges along the way to get out of this relationship, but I turned a blind eye to every single one of them. The relationship led me further and further away from Christ, and He wanted me to return to Him, but I didn't want to. The devil's grip was so strong.

On my 21st birthday, I wanted nothing more than to celebrate with Ollie. The thing is, we had broken up a couple of days prior. I honestly can't even remember why because our arguments were so frequent. However, I had already bought tickets for a dinner cruise for my birthday and asked him if he would still come since I had already spent the money. This was normal for us, breaking up but continuing communication and hanging out. I was so attached to him, I felt like we were always in a relationship, even when we broke up.

He agreed to go on my birthday cruise, but the night was horrible. All I wanted was to get back to how good things felt at the beginning of our relationship. I felt so neglected and empty. I was holding on to a relationship that should have ended years ago, but I just couldn't let go.

He could visibly tell I was upset as we drove home and returned to my apartment. Despite multiple attempts to speak to me, I ignored him. I was too emotional to talk calmly with him, so I opted for silence instead. I just wanted to change my clothes, relax for the night, and I wanted him to go home and leave me alone in peace. He didn't go home right away, though.

As I changed my clothes, I felt Ollie's presence behind me. He began to kiss me and pull on my clothes. I was baffled. How could he possibly think this was okay after he ignored me all night on the cruise? But that's how our relationship was. He always disregarded how I felt and desired to be physical instead. My brokenness led me to believe this was just his way of showing he loved me. Not this night, though; I wanted nothing to do with him.

Ollie quickly became aggressive, and I vividly recalled this side of him. It was the same aggressiveness he had in my car a few years prior. It was like he was a different person, and it scared me. Despite my saying no to Ollie's advances, once again, he didn't take no for an

answer. He was much stronger than me and only had lust on his mind. After a while, I stopped fighting back. I lay there on the bed, feeling empty and lifeless once again. This felt all too familiar to me.

I fought back the tears because he didn't use protection at all. He didn't care. The following day, I asked him for money to buy emergency contraception because he didn't use protection, but he told me he didn't have the money and that I would have to buy it myself. If you ask him, I wanted it. We were sexually active in our relationship, and sometimes even when we weren't together, so in his mind, why would this be any different?

I'll tell you the difference. I said no.

Ollie had no right to touch or have sex with me without my consent, and it took me years to call this rape. I thought it was my fault because I stayed with Ollie even after he assaulted me a second time. I continued a relationship and continued to love him. I blocked the assault from my memory and told myself it wasn't that bad. I convinced myself that I wasn't a victim of rape if I didn't fight back. Satan's lies led me to believe that this was the usual "ups and downs" of a relationship, and if I truly loved him, I would stick it out.

My dear friend, whoever you are reading this, please hear me. This is not love. This is not healthy. This is not normal. And this is not and never will be acceptable behavior. Sex without consent is rape. Period. It doesn't matter if you didn't try to fight back. It doesn't matter if you were under the influence. It doesn't matter if you love the person. It doesn't matter if you guys have had sex before. It also doesn't matter if your body reacts to it.

I'm sorry if this is too candid, but I need to be crystal clear — for those of us who are women, it does not matter if you become naturally lubricated or have an orgasm during the assault. This is your body's natural response to sexual stimulation, whether it's good or bad. And for my brothers, it does not matter if you experience an erection and ejaculation during the assault. This is also your body's natural response to sexual stimulation. This doesn't mean you deserve assault.

This is what happened to me. I convinced myself that because my body responded to the sexual stimulation, I didn't have the right to report Ollie. But what Ollie did was completely wrong, and I need people to know that without a doubt. It took me a long time to call what Ollie did "sexual abuse" and "rape." And it turns out; Ollie wasn't the first person to sexually abuse me and, unfortunately, wouldn't be the last.

Chapter 10

Shattered Souls, Part 2

B efore starting therapy, I knew something was seriously wrong. I have never hated anyone before, but something about one person, in particular, left a terrible taste in my mouth. I couldn't stand to be around them, ignored all attempts of communication, and avoided them like the plague at all costs. This person genuinely made me sick to my stomach, and I had no idea why. I felt so much conviction because I knew that, as a Christian, I shouldn't treat anyone like this. I prayed to God, asking why I felt this way. I felt so ashamed and guilty for not "loving my neighbor," as the Bible says.

Common symptoms of Post-Traumatic Stress Disorder (PTSD) are agitation, irritability, avoidance, and memory repression. Many people with PTSD can't access memories consciously because their brain protects them from the emotional pain of the trauma. However, later down the line, those repressed memories can cause psychological problems like depression and anxiety disorders. Other times, the repressed memories finally make their way to the surface, and when they do, flashbacks come rushing in like a flood.

One day, in my early college years, I was sitting at my kitchen table in my apartment, and I had a faint memory of a traumatic time when I was younger. It was very subtle, but my mind quickly flashed back to the occurrence. I was molested repeatedly, and it started when I was about 12 years old, prematurely exposing my innocent mind to sex and sexuality. I was just a child who looked up to this person and desired closeness, so I kept quiet and forgot it even happened — so I thought. Even with that fleeting memory, I convinced myself that I remembered wrong. I denied it ever happened to me.

One Sunday, after I graduated college, the person from my flashback visited me at church, and it was like my brain and body suddenly remembered everything they did to me. As a kid, I remember this person telling me they were trying to teach me how to "play house" so I'd know what to do when I was older. I believed them. They told me to go into the closet and followed behind me. After remembering this, something in me broke. I ran to the bathroom at church, having a total mental breakdown. My friend, Braxton, came rushing after me and held me in the bathroom as I sobbed in her arms. I couldn't breathe. At that moment, I knew it was finally time to get professional help. I needed to talk to someone. When I saw my therapist for the first time, I walked into the office that day with a vivid memory of why this person caused such a bad feeling in my stomach.

"I hate them," I said to my therapist, Ava.

Though I'm not proud of using the word "hate," I knew Ava had heard much worse. I talked to Ava about how I recently remembered what this person did to me as a child. I didn't want to discuss it because I had little to say. I felt bitter, numb, and cold whenever Ava asked about it.

Ava told me I didn't remember what happened to me, and I avoided talking about it because my brain had been trying to protect me for the last decade. My brain repressed the memory for over 10 years. After some tests, Ava diagnosed me with Post Traumatic Stress Disorder (PTSD). I had all the signs of it and didn't even know. I felt so much anger and emotional discord.

I repeatedly asked myself why someone would do this to me. And little did I know, this trauma carried over into other areas of my life, including my distrust for women in friendship. It all came full circle, and though it wasn't pretty, I finally had language for some of the things I felt. I finally understood why I've struggled with years of worthlessness, suicide attempts, and mental illness. I know sexual abuse isn't the only reason, but it is a massive part. I haven't confronted any of my abusers. It has taken me years to even reconcile with my history of abuse.

Statistics show that most cases of sexual abuse occur at the hands of people the victim knows. Except for a stranger who drugged and raped me, this is true for me too. I knew the others very well. Four different people all claimed parts of my body that didn't belong to them. The ramifications were broken pieces of my soul scattered everywhere. Is this all that I'm good for? I used to wonder. The perception of my value became attached to how well others could use me. Eventually, I measured my worth by how well God could use me.

I know you may think that being used by God is a good thing, right? But when you start to believe that you can earn God's love through the things you do for Him, you've missed the point of the Gospel. I tried to earn God's love and acceptance through church attendance, starting a blog and podcast, and serving. I buried myself in ministry. I thought if I proved to God that I was worthy, then He would erase these broken pieces

94

of my story and make me into someone great. I thought maybe I could forget my story of abuse if I loved God enough and served people enough. I thought maybe, just maybe, the people at church could love me back to wholeness. But guess what? It wasn't enough. In fact, it made things worse because the church I was attending at that time also had an abusive community. Not enough church and ministry in the world could put the broken pieces of my soul back together. So, I left.

After increasing conflict with Emmett and other people in my community, constant trauma triggers, and feeling like I didn't have a support system, I left the Church in 2020 for the first time since I was an infant. When I told my then-pastor why I was leaving, his response broke my heart. This was confirmation that this specific church could no longer be my place of worship. I began to believe that no place was. The COVID-19 pandemic made leaving the Church easy. No one asked questions because our state governor locked down most establishments anyway. But even after the public started opening back up, I stayed gone. I made sure I disappeared because the Church and the people that I loved so fiercely suddenly felt like they didn't love me back.

Church scandal surfaced in the outside world, division came, and I no longer recognized this faith that raised me. The Church looked more like the people who abused me than it did the beautiful bride of Christ, and I hated it. I hated myself. I had to get out. But without a church, my community, or singing as a worship leader, I didn't know what to do with myself. I didn't know who I was outside of those things. And I was no longer sure that I believed in the Christian faith. It hurt too much.

I started to develop trust issues, particularly with Christian men in leadership. I questioned whether I was even a Christian.

I honestly felt that if these prominent Christian leaders were living in sin and my old church was overlooking sin, then undoubtedly, small Jordyn must have no concept of what it means to live as a Christian at all. I questioned my own salvation, and it hurt so badly. Everything I thought I knew felt like a lie.

I tried to think of an explanation for why I believed in God and couldn't come up with one. I couldn't give an account for my faith (1 Peter 3:15), and this scared me. How could I have gone all these years quoting Scripture, praying, and reading my Bible and not be able to defend my faith? Did I ever truly believe in God? Had my entire faith been a lie? Much of what I thought about the Bible hinged on what a preacher told me, not personal pursuit. Because of this, I officially entered an existential crisis.

The enemy had a field day with my doubts. I came across YouTube videos of ex-missionaries who were now agnostics and everything of the sort. I wrestled with God and asked Him for answers but felt like He was silent. And it wasn't like I didn't believe in God. I knew I believed in Him; I just wasn't sure *why*. And I assume He was silent because He couldn't tell me why I believed in Him. That was something for me to answer on my own.

So, I stumbled around trying to answer it on my own by deconstructing my faith. Abuse and rejection from people in the Church made me look at myself and everything else around me through a broken lens. So, I knew that if I wanted to see God's heart in this colossal mess, I had to tear down what I assumed to be "good Christian" behavior and instead rebuild my faith on the foundation of one thing: the good news of Jesus Christ. My faith wouldn't stand a chance if I continued to place it in other people's actions. Because the truth is, none of us are good enough.

Up until this point, I didn't realize how much my upbringing pruned me to be a "good Christian girl." My life followed one simple formula: do "X" correctly and get rewarded with "Y." Except that formula isn't simple at all. It shaped me to seek validation in broken ways because I desired to be loved, admired, and seen as worthy. And it carried over into my relationship with Jesus. All I had to do was follow the rules, complete the formula, and life would be okay, right? Wrong. Very wrong.

Even after hearing the Gospel repeatedly, I still tried to earn God's love and favor. The need to overwork and overproduce fueled my desire to be proven worthy to God and others. I wanted people to like me. I wanted them to choose me. To see me. To value me. So, I followed the rules. But all rules get broken at some point.

I knew I couldn't and shouldn't wrestle with such a magnitude of doubts on my own, so I reached out to an old college mentor. Let's call him DJ. Back in college, I was in a ministry led by DJ that changed my life. Though I had grown up in church, I had never experienced a Christian leader so honest and vulnerable as DJ. I was used to pastors and bishops in clergy collars walking around preaching against sin without ever acknowledging their own. They never talked about their brokenness. But DJ was different.

He stood in front of a room full of impressionable college kids and talked about his weaknesses. He talked about his sin, which I'm sure wasn't easy because, as his students, we could have looked at him as if he was in no place to be leading us, but we didn't. You couldn't help but see how Jesus radically

97

changed his heart. I knew it wasn't fake. In wrestling with my questions and doubts about Christianity, I knew DJ was who I wanted to talk to.

I gave him a call, and he immediately made time for me. We attended church together, grabbed brunch afterward, and I poured my heart out to him. I told him I was lost, confused, and hurt. I told him I had doubts about being a Christian and how I felt like I'd been getting it wrong this whole time. And you know what DJ did? He cried with me right at the table. He apologized to me on behalf of those who hurt me. And at that moment, I knew God had been keeping track of my sorrow and collecting every one of my tears in his jar (Psalm 56:8).

If DJ, a flawed human man, could feel my sorrow and meet it with compassion, how much more could my Creator, the divine God of the universe, be feeling on my behalf? He empathizes even more because he knows exactly what it feels like to be rejected, abandoned, and abused. He came down to earth, was born as a baby, and was placed in a box meant to feed animals. He was hated and disrespected. People beat him, spat on him, and he was crucified, dying a criminal's death though innocent, all because he loves me. And loves you, too.

There was my answer. This became my *why*.

Why do I believe in God? Why do I believe He sent His only Son, Jesus Christ, to die for my sins? Because I have never felt love like this. I have never felt a hand so comforting or heard a voice so gentle. I have never experienced such grace that can see me at my worst and still love me. Despite all the heartbreak, depression, suicide attempts, pain, sin, mistakes, and disappointments, He never stopped coming after me. No matter how far away I drifted, He remained constant and steadfast. And He still does, every single day. He doesn't do any of this because of anything I have done or will do because, quite frankly, it'll never be enough, but it's because of God's matchless love, grace, and mercy.

Do I have all the answers? No, I don't. I have no idea when planet Earth came into existence or if dinosaurs walked the earth with humans. I have no idea what angels really look like. I have no idea what tomorrow holds, and I certainly have no idea why He loves us the way that He does. But I think that's the point.

We seem to lose the art of wonder the older we get. As wide-eyed children, it's so easy to look at a massive tree, point up at it, and say, "Whoa," and nothing else. Children don't struggle with pride or tireless ambition. Maybe this is why Jesus said that if we don't become like children, then we won't enter the kingdom of heaven (Matthew 18:3). This is not to say they don't have questions; they certainly do. But their questions are not based on the need to feel greater or stronger than they are. They just marvel at the world around them. Many kids get to be carefree.

I know this isn't everyone's story. It certainly wasn't mine. I didn't grow up in a two-parent loving household. I didn't have a dad at home to teach me how to ride a bike or clean up my cuts when I fell. I didn't have people to protect me from the abuse I endured. I didn't have the emotional support I needed growing up. And I had many times where I asked why. Many times, the pity for myself was so great that I didn't see the point in living anymore. But God.

He stepped in as the emotional security I longed for. He continues to protect me and teach me. He disciplines me in the holiest way. He comforts and rocks me to sleep when anxiety and depression try to cripple me. And it turns out that's enough for me. I have realized that I don't need all the answers to live a life of freedom or walk out my faith. God is big enough for my questions and sovereign enough to keep some things to himself until it's time to reveal them. There is beauty in the unknown when you surrender to the only true and living God.

At the beginning of this book, I said I didn't know who this was for, but I knew someone out there needed these pages. Even *I* needed these pages. I don't know who you are or your story. I don't know the pain and sorrow you have endured. If no one ever said sorry or showed you compassion, I sincerely apologize from the bottom of my heart. I'm so sorry about what happened to you. I'm sorry people hurt and abandoned you. And I'm so sorry you've been trying to nurse yourself back to health all alone. I know how confusing, lonely, and life-altering pain can be. If you were a victim of abuse, please know it wasn't your fault. If people reject you because of your mistakes, please know that God can redeem anything and make it new, including you.

In 2 Corinthians 12:7, the Apostle Paul talks about a "thorn" in his side. The Bible doesn't tell us exactly what the thorn in Paul's side was. It could have been a physical illness or even a mental one. It could have been the persecution he was facing. We aren't given the details. But we do know these three things: the thorn caused Paul pain, the thorn was put there by Satan, and Paul begged God to take it away, but God said no.

Take a little time to read 2 Corinthians 12:7-10. Why do you think God wouldn't remove this painful thorn from Paul's side? I believe it's because God wanted Paul to stay submitted and surrendered to Him. God told Paul that his grace was more than enough to get him through this pain.

"My grace is all you need. My power works best in weakness," says God.

I can't even begin to tell you how many times, much like Paul, I begged God to take all my pain away. I wish I could say I am above a temper tantrum, but I'm not. I've screamed and cried at God. I've questioned His love for me and expressed how angry I was at Him for letting certain things happen to me. I've thrown myself plenty of pity parties.

I won't lie to you, life can really hurt sometimes, but I've finally gotten to a place where I feel like Paul in this passage. Now, "…I am glad to boast about my weaknesses, so that the power of Christ can work through me" (2 Corinthians 12:9). Without my past experiences, I don't believe I would have ever been able to write this book. I also don't think I would have truly come to know Jesus.

God could have easily and quickly taken this thorn away from Paul — he's God. And if you're anything like me, you didn't understand why an all-powerful God would let His child feel pain. But I think without pain, we would never learn how to rely on God. We would never learn how to give our pain over to Him and lean into His grace. Without pain, we would never know God as our Healer, Comforter, or true Friend.

Many years later, I'm still on the couch — my therapist's couch. I'm convinced that God's holiness rests on this couch. Why? Because only a true and living God can use a couch and a woman sitting across from it to heal the wounds that should have killed me. My abusive experiences caused a lot of damage. I also caused a lot of damage. I hurt people because I was hurting myself.

When I began to explore the hurt with my therapist, each conversation led me to a new level of healing. One where the Almighty feels the abuse with me and the holes in His hands ache. One where the King of Glory touches each place in my body that holds trauma and gives it purpose. One where even though these thorns in my side are incredibly painful, the blood that dripped from Jesus' hands and feet on the cross covers it all. Some people hate that roses have thorns, but I, for one, am grateful the thorns have roses.

Even when it doesn't *feel* like it, friend, I promise His grace is enough.

JORDYN IMARI is a Christian author, blogger, and Emotional Intelligence Coach. She helps women who are stuck in a cycle of pain heal their emotional wounds so they can experience deeper, more meaningful relationships with Jesus and others.

Jordyn Imari uses her personal testimony to fuel and create content that cultivates healing in others. As someone who endured trauma and abuse that made her question her value and faith, Jordyn is passionate about the intersection of emotional health and spirituality and uses her creativity as a safe space to explore both.

Jordyn has written for Freed Magazine and The Truly Co. She is also the author of Peace, Love, and Prayer: A Prayer Journal for Millennials. Jordyn calls Ohio home, and you can usually catch her in a local coffee shop with a chai tea latte in hand.

Connect with Jordyn:

Website: www.jordynimari.com
Instagram: @jordynimari

www.ingramcontent.com/pod-product-compliance
Lightning Source LLC
Chambersburg PA
CBHW020208090426
42734CB00008B/986